Beyond Words

Beyond Words

Philosophy, Fiction, and the Unsayable

Timothy Cleveland

LEXINGTON BOOKS
Lanham • Boulder • New York • London

Published by Lexington Books
An imprint of The Rowman & Littlefield Publishing Group, Inc.
4501 Forbes Boulevard, Suite 200, Lanham, Maryland 20706
www.rowman.com

86-90 Paul Street, London EC2A 4NE

Copyright © 2022 by The Rowman & Littlefield Publishing Group, Inc.

Epigraph: Alighieri, Dante. *The Divine Comedy, Paradiso*. Translated by Charles S. Singleton. Princeton University Press, 1991.

All rights reserved. No part of this book may be reproduced in any form or by any electronic or mechanical means, including information storage and retrieval systems, without written permission from the publisher, except by a reviewer who may quote passages in a review.

British Library Cataloguing in Publication Information Available

Library of Congress Cataloging-in-Publication Data

Names: Cleveland, Timothy, author.
Title: Beyond words : philosophy, fiction, and the unsayable / Timothy Cleveland.
Description: Lanham : Lexington Books, [2022] | Includes bibliographical references and index. | Summary: "Beyond Words argues that some works of fiction and poetry are especially, perhaps even best, suited to expanding our awareness and understanding into the nature of things otherwise unsayable and unconceived. Such literary works do philosophy, showing us something that a theoretical-scientific or philosophical-discourse cannot literally say"-- Provided by publisher.
Identifiers: LCCN 2022024148 (print) | LCCN 2022024149 (ebook) | ISBN 9781793614841 (cloth) | ISBN 9781793614865 (paperback) | ISBN 9781793614858 (ebook)
Subjects: LCSH: Ineffable, The, in literature. | Literature--Philosophy. | Fiction--History and criticism--Theory, etc. | Poetry--History and criticism--Theory, etc. | LCGFT: Literary criticism.
Classification: LCC PN56.I59 C47 2022 (print) | LCC PN56.I59 (ebook) | DDC 809/.93384--dc23/eng/20220714
LC record available at https://lccn.loc.gov/2022024148
LC ebook record available at https://lccn.loc.gov/2022024149

For

Brenda

beloved beyond words

Trasumanar significar per verba

non si poria; però l'essemplo basti

a cui esperïenza grazia serba.

. . . passing beyond humanity may not be set forth in words: therefore let the example suffice any for whom grace reserves that experience.

—Dante, *Paradiso*, Canto I

Contents

Preface	xi
Introduction: Encountering the Unsayable	1
Chapter 1: The Platonic Paradigm	9
Chapter 2: The Experience of the Unsayable	25
Chapter 3: The In Principle Ineffable and the Trivially Ineffable	39
Chapter 4: Showing What Can Be Said	59
Chapter 5: Showing What Cannot Be Said	83
Conclusion	109
Bibliography	113
Index	119
About the Author	125

Preface

Trying to write a book on the unsayable seems a self-defeating endeavor, bound to fail. To say something about the unsayable not only seems paradoxical but an obvious contradiction. To put into words something about the limits of our words and bounds of language seems possible if not more palatable. It is the task I have taken on along with all the conceptual risks that come with it.

Saying the unsayable certainly sounds incoherent on the face of it, but we are often struck by the feeling that some things are beyond words. The familiar phrase is part of our everyday speech. Someone says, "How much I appreciate what you've done for me is *beyond words*," and we will immediately understand this to mean, "I cannot put into words or express in words how much I appreciate your work." The phrase "beyond words" in ordinary, everyday speech means something that words can't articulate or say. The ordinary connotation of the phrase is to express the limits of our words and that something is unsayable. To say something that I feel or experience is beyond words does not ring incoherent. On the contrary, it is an expression we use to convey our reaction to some experience, say one we had at a concert, in church, or at a museum. The way a work of art strikes us, the feel of a religious or spiritual revelation are often considered beyond words.

I am confident that these claims are not only coherent, they are also true sometimes. Those feelings that resist expression may be most acutely discerned, even if faintly understood. It is far from rare when the most profound experiences not only struggle against but withstand words. We do experience things unsayable, at least some of us do. Another place where I think this occurs is in the literary arts. Some works of fiction and poetry show us something beyond words. In these cases, it is words showing the limits of words. Moreover, when literary works accomplish this, they provide philosophical insight or understanding. They contribute to philosophy in only a way fiction or poetry can. Though these claims sound more controversial and difficult to defend, I have long believed them from my youth. That is why I wrote this book. To try to articulate why what I have long felt is true. I believe that this can be successfully done. I hope I have managed that to some extent herein.

This task combines two of my great passions—philosophy and literature. In college, I threw off the last vestiges of the Southern Baptist faith I was reared in and gradually replaced it with a new faith in philosophy. Philosophy, as I was taught it, was concerned with giving reasons, reasons for our most basic beliefs and assumptions that put the world together for us. Its reasons could yield understanding. But philosophy, with all its promise, was not my first love, literature was. I remember in grade school reading an E. E. Cummings' poem about the moon being a balloon, and it still brings me wonder. Before you gaze again at the full moon, read that poem. You'll never look at the moon the same again. I know I never will.

Though fiction and poetry are not a matter of reasons and arguments, I have always considered the literature and philosophy of a piece. Early in my college career I was allowed to take an advanced English class on the American novel. Among the works we read was William Faulkner's *The Sound and the Fury*. In the few days I had to read it I was mesmerized. I couldn't put it down. When I slept I dreamed it—Dilsey and the Compsons, Benjy, Quentin, Jason all in my head, and I in theirs. The experience was visceral and even then, before I could have ever articulated why, I knew there was something deeply philosophical about it. I feel it every time I read the book. That is another reason I wanted to write this book—to show why I think these two great passions of mine make a beautiful union. For me, I am sure they will never part.

I have always felt that my best contribution to philosophy was not in my work, not in anything I have written, but is the many exceptional students I have had the privilege to teach. So it was especially rewarding to be able to have had the help of my friend and former student Brandon Tyler throughout this project. Since his student days, he and I have had in-depth conversations covering everything from philosophy and religion to literature and film. He took my class on philosophy and literature, and we have been talking about the ideas in this book ever since. I think I may have learned more from him than he from me. These conversations have had an invaluable impact on this book. I am especially grateful to his very insightful discussions of the works of Stanley Cavell and William Faulkner and especially the films of Terrence Malick. He has read the manuscript more times than anyone, perhaps even me, and has been an amazing copy editor. This work has been much improved by his help on it. I cannot thank him enough.

My friend and colleague Mark Walker has been an immense influence. Mark and I have had many conversations about my thoughts on philosophy and literature. He always opens my mind to new ways to think of things. He convinced me to put my argument in terms of semantic expansion. It is based on that idea that the main philosophical case for the unsayable is made. It was Mark's encouragement and confidence in me that inspired me finally to sit down and try to put my ideas in words. I am truly grateful for all his help.

I would like to thank another former student, colleague, and friend, Jean-Paul Vessel, who read earlier bits of this and gave me perceptive and very helpful comments especially on Plato and his quarrel with the poets. We have had many conversations over the years about these topics. I owe several of the examples in the book to discussions with him.

I would like to thank Vince Colapietro, Kristina Grob, and Kyle Bromhall for helpful comments and discussion of talks where I presented early versions of some of these ideas. Their comments all helped me refine and formulate the ideas that were to become this book.

I owe a debt to an anonymous reviewer who made a number of insightful remarks and suggestions that guided my revisions and greatly improved the final version.

My editor at Lexington, Jana Hodges-Kluck, has been a pleasure to work with at every stage of this process. I greatly appreciate the belief she has shown in my work from the beginning, her constructive suggestions, and all her help.

I am honored that my friend Michael Poncé allowed me to use one of his paintings from his Waste Land series for the cover. He is an artist whose style and sensibility makes him perfect at capturing Eliot's poem on canvas.

Finally, and most importantly, to my wife, Brenda, without you it is no exaggeration to say I would have never done this work. Your love and support are my greatest blessing. You are my angel and muse. It is to you this book is dedicated.

Introduction
Encountering the Unsayable

Paintings, pictures, and photographs often strike us as showing something indescribable. They suggest to us some complex emotion or feeling we cannot put into words. Think of the paintings of Rothko, Picasso, Jackson Pollock, portraits by Da Vinci and Vermeer. Music can also have that effect, Shostakovich's 7th symphony, the late piano sonatas of Beethoven, solos by Miles Davis or John Coltrane. It may not be much of a stretch to think some films do the same. Films are after all moving pictures accompanied often by music. They usually include words as well, so perhaps it is a bit more of a stretch. There are some powerful films that serve as strong contenders for showing something that cannot be said. Terrence Malick's film *The Thin Red Line* depicts the horrors of war in a breathtaking story of the battle of Guadalcanal. But it is far from a traditional war film. It is in no way nationalistic; it does not take sides. There is no glory in war or camaraderie among a band of brothers. No one wins. The war scenes depict only havoc and seemingly pointless anguish. The film is structured in fragmentary scenes, unordered in time. The beauty of the images and the graphic horrors seem at odds, yet the paradoxical combination somehow works. It not only works; the magic of this masterpiece would not work in any other way. The film presents a philosophical reflection on the nature of evil and its presence in the world. We hear it in the voice-over narration and the characters' dialogue. On the face of it, these words ask philosophical questions that the film attempts to answer. Yet this simple way of approaching it may well miss how Malick's film works and the power of what it pulls off.

The critics Leo Bersani and Ulysse Dutoit suggest that it presents a response that cannot be put in words: "Language raises questions which, Malick's film suggests, language may be inherently unable to answer." Instead, "the film's response will be non-discursive."[1] The words spoken in the film function less to raise literal questions, but "more as a kind of musical voice motif than as discursive formulations that might be addressed philosophically."[2] The repetition of questions function as a refrain. The images and scenes respond visually.[3] There are many close shots of faces that call our attention to the mystery of their expressions. For Bersani and Dutoit these looks are like cameras through which the characters register the world. The faces represent ways of looking at the world. Each character displays a subjective point of view. We see their world on their faces. The film turns this idea on itself. The camera is not an objective way to capture the world but treated by Malick as another subjective lens. This technique undermines the camera's objective standpoint and it becomes our subjective perspective on the world of good and evil. We witness the fragmented experiences of war and violence juxtaposed with natural beauty. We are dislocated. The voice-over lags just behind or ahead of the images. We are unsure where it is coming from and often who is speaking. Yet the voice is always in some sense tied to what we are seeing, even if it is unclear or paradoxical how. These scenes show us the complexities of our moral reality. The immediate visual experience of these scenes gives us direct moral insight that transcends the distinctions the philosophical questions presupposed. The film bestows a moral insight that cannot be put in words. My description of the film and how it works and achieves its effect is sayable, but the philosophical response the film elicits is not.

The response is experienced, and this experience is a result of the form of the film, the way in which the various elements are formally related. This kind of understanding seems plausible for a film such as *The Thin Red Line* in a way it doesn't for a literary work. A film is directly experienced. *The Thin Red Line* will still have a visceral effect even if you don't understand English and have no subtitles. Any experienced understanding of a literary work seems mediated by an understanding of the words. For a particular film to show what cannot be discursively said seems almost as natural as it does for some paintings, pictures, or pieces of music. For works of fiction and poetry, which consist of words, this understanding seems much less plausible. The sense of words is independent of pictures and picturing. Though I do not endorse Wittgenstein's picture theory of meaning any more than he ultimately did, I do want to argue that sometimes a literary work can show what cannot be said. When it does, the formal features of the work depict in a way much like a picture. Literary works that do this contribute to philosophy just as Malick's film provides an unsayable philosophical response.

I used words to describe Malick's film but not the experience it brings. My point is to the contrary. The experience is unsayable. It defies description. Sometimes if we try too hard to put the experience that works of fiction, poetry, and film lend, we lose the experience altogether. Too much talk overintellectualizes the work, kills the art. Writers often cringe when critics armed with too much theory or ideology talk about their work. David Foster Wallace compares his reaction to a description of how students are taught standard literary analysis: "This is a lot like the teacher's feeling at running a Kafka story through the gears of your standard undergrad-course literary analysis—plot to chart, symbols to decode, etc. Kafka, of course, would be in a unique position to appreciate the irony of submitting his short stories to this kind of high-efficiency critical machine."[4] The theory or ideology provides the critic with a conceptual formula with which to pin down the meaning of the works and utterly destroys the experience. Wallace aptly says it is "the literary equivalent to tearing the petals off and grinding them up and running the goo through a spectrometer to explain why a rose smells so pretty."[5] We have all encountered this phenomenon at some time or other. Our recoil at such analyses is evidence that we feel that some works are showing us something that cannot be said. A similar point can be made about jokes. We all know someone who has tried to retell a joke and by describing it made it very unfunny. Imagine a twenty-page Freudian analysis of a Dave Chappelle joke. It would not only most certainly miss the meaning but it would definitely ruin the comic effect.

Such analyses do not exactly abound for jokes. Probably because if they did, no one would take them seriously. But there are plenty of examples for fiction and poetry. Don DeLillo's novel *Underworld* has been the object of some. Consider this passage about the novel's key moment when we discover what haunts the main character, Nick—his accidental shooting of his friend years before:

> Nick's oedipal narrative stalls at this moment of aporia; repetition does not lead to mastery, but to domination by the trajectory of trauma. Nick's repetition compulsion suggests a subjectivity that has internalized the effects of alterity, has turned the eruption of the real upon itself, has embraced the death instinct 'beyond the pleasure principle.' Yet the larger narrative of the novel, which circles the absent center of the cultural imaginary and symbolic—atomic trauma—is more successful. For the impossible kernel of traumatic alterity, and its inescapable excess, are integral to the structure of the novel.[6]

That this description doesn't exactly capture the artistic effectiveness of the moment seems an understatement. Indeed, it seems to do violence to it. Reading this analysis, we would never know that the novel has been praised for its emotional power. Though I will say a considerable amount about how novels, stories, and poems show the unsayable, I will never attempt to describe the experience. Quite the contrary. My whole point is that they can only be shown, pointed to. For these literary works to do that, there always comes a time when we must stop talking. We must remain silent. My advice without fail is read the work. Only then will you know the experience, know what it shows.

It is commonplace to regard many great works of literature—poems, dramas, fictions—as in some sense philosophical, yet ever since Plato there has been a tension between the kind of abstract theorizing that goes on in philosophy and the kind of focus on concrete particulars that occurs in poetry and fiction. I want to elaborate on and address this Platonic tension and ask in what sense, if any, literature in the form of poetry, drama, short stories, and novels can contribute significantly to our philosophical understanding. Ultimately, I will suggest there is something in the form or the style of certain poems, novels, and stories that makes them especially, perhaps even best suited to expanding our awareness and understanding into the nature of things otherwise unsayable and unconceived of. So such literary works *do* philosophy. Literary texts may show us something that a theoretical—scientific or philosophical—discourse cannot literally say.

Thus this book defends two bold claims: First, there are things that are, in some philosophically, non-trivial sense, unsayable. They can only be shown not said; and second, some great literary texts show us—provide us with insight into or a kind of knowledge of—the unsayable. A significant meta-philosophical conclusion follows from the defense of these two claims: there are limits to the insights that the philosophical method, traditionally conceived, can provide. These are the unsayable philosophical insights that some great literary works show us. In order to defend these claims, I will have to take a stand on controversial issues at the intersection of epistemology, philosophy of mind, philosophy of language, philosophy of science, aesthetics, and philosophy of literature. At each of these points, the discussion could have delved into any number of contentious details. Interesting philosophical investigations often bog down in such minutiae. I think it more important first to lay the groundwork. Think of this book as a philosophical prolegomena to fiction and the unsayable.

I use the term 'fiction' in a very broad sense, certainly broader than the person on the street. I will speak of fiction and sometimes include poetry and plays. In Plato's day, fiction and drama were both poetry. Today we are careful to distinguish them, though dramas are sometimes still written in verse and poetry is usually full of the techniques of fiction. I do not believe we can provide a very sharp delineation of these that keeps them necessarily distinct. The genres blend into each other. At best, we can define them by ostension, pointing to paradigm cases. They can all fall sometimes into what I am calling 'fiction.' Poetry, drama, novels, and short stories have in common that their artistic aim is not restrained by, nor directed at, the expression of literal truths. They are all fabrications and in that sense fictions. So, I will loosely include them all as fictions; that is, these genres all have cases that clearly fall into fiction, as I will understand it. Sometimes I will call them 'the fictive literary arts.' I will speak of them also, even more loosely, as the literary arts, ignoring that much nonfiction writing, including philosophy, is literary. At times I do this simply for stylistic variety. I will let context dictate my intent.

I use the term 'unsayable' in a less broad sense. In today's popular parlance, the word 'unsayable' means something unspeakable in the sense of being too horrible, either morally or otherwise, to talk about. Of course, I do not intend any such connotation. I take the word 'unsayable' in Wittgenstein's sense of *Unaussprechliches* and use it interchangeably with 'inexpressible,' and 'ineffable.' The unsayable is something beyond words, beyond what language can express. The usual contenders for the unsayable are religious revelations and aesthetic experiences of, as I mention above, paintings and pieces of music. I will suggest others in the course of this book.

The book divides into roughly two parts. The first three chapters sketch the philosophical framework, the last two provide readings of philosophical literary works within this framework. They all are necessary to present my view and argue for it, the literary readings as well as the philosophical arguments. The case is not complete until it is clear that specific works of fiction and poetry can contribute to philosophy, that literary arts can do philosophy and not simply illustrate it.

In chapter 1, I will take up Plato's quarrel with the poets and argue that his legacy persists. There is a vast and controversial literature concerning what Plato really thought about the poets. I will simply provide a sketch to explain how Plato discovered something perhaps necessary to theoretical understanding, both scientific and philosophical, that is still with us. If so, it remains one of the compelling reasons for denying that fictions can make serious contributions to philosophy proper. However, if poetry, plays, novels, and short stories can in a non-trivial sense show the unsayable, this aspect of theorizing that Plato recognized will not prevent these literary arts from sometimes making contributions to philosophy.

The very idea of showing the unsayable in words borders on paradoxical. In chapter 2, I take up what candidates there could be for something unsayable. What could we be aware of that is inexpressible? I argue that a good candidate is our first-person knowledge of our own sense experiences and other immediate states of consciousness. The direct, non-propositional knowledge by acquaintance we have of these is a paradigm case, if there are any, of something unsayable. Knowledge by acquaintance of our immediate states of consciousness may be something that is unsayable that poetry and fiction can sometimes show us. But what we know by direct acquaintance and what poetry and fiction can show with words seem at odds. Knowledge of what it is like to have a particular experience is first-person knowledge. It is subjective. But the words of poetry and fiction are third-person, objective. They can be shared, unlike a first-person experience. So how can poetry or fiction show us what an experience is like? To address this worry, I will employ Stanley Cavell's distinction between knowing and acknowledging. Poetry and fiction may show us something unsayable we recognize from first-person experience. As a result, we acknowledge in others what we cannot know by ourselves. The works exhibit a state of consciousness that we recognize as other than our own and acknowledge subjects of experience other than ourselves. Some philosophers suspect that what it is like to have an experience is only trivially ineffable and so not philosophically interesting. Perhaps what renders it trivial is that this aspect of sense experience is ineffable only by definition. I will raise serious doubts about this claim.

Philosophers generally assume that any philosophically interesting case of something unsayable would have to be unsayable in principle, not simply in practice. The latter cases are philosophically trivial. I scrutinize this distinction in chapter 3 and argue that it does not distinguish the philosophically interesting from the philosophically trivial. Whether there is anything unsayable in principle seems to depend on the nature of language. If the nature of language sets limits to what can be said, then there will be things beyond that limit it cannot express. If there are no in principle limits, it seems what is unsayable is only so in practice. It is unsayable only at the time. I argue that we may not be able to determine whether language has limited expressibility, but that it does not matter. Either way, this investigation will leave us with a philosophically interesting sense of the unsayable. The philosophically significant unsayable need not be inexpressible in principle. This conclusion will help explain how fiction can do philosophy by showing the unsayable.

There are, of course, plenty of philosophers who think fictions can do philosophy. They reject the Platonic conception in one way or other. Among these are philosophers of a pragmatic stripe. In chapter 4, I find instructive a recent suggestion by Philip Kitcher. For him, we should take fictions seriously as philosophy. To do so, he thinks we must abandon the dominant model of philosophy as restricted to carefully reasoned arguments from well-justified premises. The philosophy done by some great novels is in the showing not saying. I concur, but I argue that the kind of showing that he counts as philosophy neither shows something unsayable, nor is it outside the conception of philosophy as the critical reflection on, and refinement of, our beliefs through careful reasoning and the evaluation of arguments. Some works of fiction and poetry do philosophy, and the philosophy is in the showing, not the saying. But they show something expressible in discursive terms. To punctuate this point and distinguish this view from my own, I will consider two literary works. The first is a careful reading of Herman Melville's novella, *Billy Budd,* as philosophy. I argue that it works, at least in part, as a powerful philosophical thought experiment. If so, this is a way fiction can contribute to philosophy. The second case comes from Harryette Mullen's book of poetry, *Sleeping with the Dictionary.* The unique syntactic and semantic innovations of her poems unmask our presuppositions about language and the world represented in our linguistic practices and everyday speech. It shows us something, but what it shows can be said. The idea that a novel or a poem could, in words, express the unsayable is left paradoxical and elusive.

Chapter 5 offers readings of three literary works: T. S. Eliot's poem *The Waste Land*, Charles Baxter's short story "Snow," and William Faulkner's novel *The Sound and the Fury*. All of these succeed in showing something unsayable. Much like *The Thin Red Line*, what they show is a result of the formal features or structure of these works. Eliot considered Dante the greatest philosophical poet, the poet who best did philosophy through poetry. In his poetry he found a way to pass beyond the limits of humanity and show us his revelation of the divine. Eliot's interpretation will be one key to understanding fiction and poetry as philosophy. The other key will recall Cavell's distinction between knowing and acknowledging. Together they will open the door of philosophy Plato closed to poetry and fiction.

In the end, I return to where I started and wonder how Plato might have settled the ancient quarrel differently and wonder what so settling it might have done for him and his philosophical project. And I will suggest what it might do for us.

NOTES

1. Leo Bersani and Ulysse Dutoit, "'One Big Soul' (*The Thin Red Line*)," in *Forms of Being* (London: British Film Institute, 2004), 134.
2. Ibid., 138.
3. Ibid., 143.
4. David Foster Wallace, "Laughing with Kafka," *Log*, no. 22, The Absurd (Spring/Summer 2011): 47–50.
5. Ibid.
6. Leonard Wilcox, "Don DeLillo's *Underworld* and the Return of the Real," *Contemporary Literature* 43, no. 1 (Spring, 2002): 120–37, 132.

Chapter 1

The Platonic Paradigm

Imagine Plato were successful in establishing his republic.[1] The poets have been exiled, long ago escorted out the city gates. The 'ancient quarrel' between philosophy and poetry is now ancient history. Philosophy victorious. Logic and reasoned argument provide the ultimate justification for belief and action. Homer, Sappho, Aeschylus, Sophocles, Euripides, and Aristophanes are beyond recollection, banished from the books. A few lines may have survived, passed down by word of mouth, but the state, and the philosophers who run it, allow them only insofar as they are used for rational purposes, if that is possible. Some citizens may quote these lines from time to time in conversation—the scattered remains of oral history—but they are unaware of the original contexts, ignorant as they are of the great works from which they come. They have no clue who actually wrote them. These random lines, amputated as they are from works left to die, lose all their original meaning and power. There are no poets left, remembered or otherwise. The history of poetry and fictional literature as we know it ends there. The novel never comes into being. Lyric poetry is no more, never to reach its prominence. Indeed, the modern pop song as a form of poetic expression cannot emerge. Rap, never to be allowed on the streets, will not erupt on the scene. It, like all these forms of poetry and fictional drama, are simply too dangerous to the survival of the just state and the stability of the tranquility it offers. This republic flourishes in many ways. Logic and mathematics evolve constantly and smoothly to their present zenith, as do the science and technology their development helps make possible. The king is a philosopher who rules the state in a perfectly rational fashion. Every citizen, educated according to its cognitive capacities, has its right place in society. For, most importantly, this republic is a just state. Moreover, though there are no more poets or poetry, a kind of fictional literature—myth—not only remains but is allowed and sanctioned by the state. After all, some people, due to their limited cognitive development, cannot be persuaded to rational ends by well-reasoned arguments and logic. Stories, deliberate fictions, are used to move those people to their rational ends. So, fiction survives in the form of myth, but only those myths underwritten by reason and the state. The urge may still arise in some to write creatively, free of the constraints of logic and dialectic method. These artistic urges will have to be repressed and sublimated into a different form of expression. Some of these forms of expression may indeed be dark, violent, and criminal, and likewise be forbidden. Some citizens may yet keep diaries or notebooks for personal artistic expression, but much of the inspiration and purpose of this kind of writing will have been lost, having left town with the last of the poets. However, some of these artistic urges will find sublimated expression in scientific innovation, technological invention, commercial industry, and expert craftsmanship. There will be venues aplenty to channel artistic expression. Such a compromise in creativity may seem a reasonable price to pay for a perfectly just state. But what exactly is the cost? What is lost in this triumph of philosophical method?

There are, of course, the obvious losses—all the world's great literature, a loss of massive intrinsic value, as well as the psychological impact of being deprived of the enjoyment and stimulation it would bring and the medium for personal expression it would provide. These costs are great enough, but in sheer *philosophical* terms, the damage may be much worse, or so I want to suggest. Here's why. Plato's fear of the poets came, in part, from the threat they posed to the scope of reason and the method of dialectic. Plato's revolutionary intellectual insight gleaned from Socrates was to recognize a goal for philosophy and spell out a method for reaching it. The goal of philosophy is knowledge—of one's self, the world, and society. The method is to subject our beliefs about these matters to rigorous scrutiny, defending our beliefs with reason and arguments. Those beliefs that cannot pass this test must be abandoned. The result of such self-knowledge and knowledge of the world will be an understanding of the good life, of what is really valuable. Knowledge of social matters will give us comprehensive insight into what makes a just social arrangement, the perfect state. That is why philosophers, masters of this dialectical method, should rule.

But I am afraid that the very success of this method with its banishing of the poets and the banning of all poetic fashion might actually be self-defeating, undermining its own ends. What would be cut off along with the poets, and all forms of creative expression that sprung from them, is an avenue of innovative expression crucial to discovery, understanding, and knowledge. What would be denied us is not only a unique, possibly irreplaceable way of forging new syntactic, semantic, and conceptual ground, but also all forms of fictional, non-literal expression which depend on a kind of linguistic creativity that constantly pushes the bounds of language. Lost would be a crucial way of expanding the language into new linguistic and conceptual territory, and sometimes pointing beyond the bounds to reveal something literally inexpressible, certainly at the time, if not forever, ineffable. This route to the growth of knowledge would be forfeited.

What is the point of my melodramatic, anachronistic caricature? It did not happen, it never would have, nor could it have. We now live in a world rich with poetry, drama, and fiction that is the latest stage in a fertile history of a language flourishing with artistic literary expression. We value that history and our freedom of expression. Nonetheless, in that same world, the dominant understanding of the discipline of philosophy has carved a domain that has marginalized the literary arts—poetry, drama, and fiction—not as a valuable source of aesthetic experience and enjoyment, but as a serious contributor to philosophy. I think part of the reason for this split is that Plato discovered something about the nature of theoretical understanding that is still with us, and remains compelling, perhaps inevitable. Philosophy, in the dominant tradition the Greeks handed down to us, is the activity of critically reflecting on and scrutinizing our basic beliefs. If literature affords us insights and knowledge that philosophy cannot articulate because it is unsayable in literal terms, then it is a threat to the comprehensive, exclusive role of philosophy and philosophers as guides to the good life and creating the best society. This possibility is something Plato would definitely have feared and done his best to criticize and expel from his republic. But I think we should not. There are things we can know or have insight into that are literally unsayable in a theoretical discourse. Great literary texts—poems, novels, dramas—sometimes show us something that theoretical discourse cannot, in a non-trivial sense, say. Literature can, and often does, enlighten us. Sometimes this takes the form of showing us that which cannot literally be said. One region of literature's domain is the unsayable. The insight that it affords us into that aspect of reality alone should count as philosophy. So I will argue.

PLATO AND THE POETS

Plato is infamous for banning poets from his republic. For him, poetry springs from a kind of divine madness at odds with philosophical method. In his early dialogue *Ion*, Socrates interrogates Ion on the nature of poetry. Ion, who is a well-known reciter of poems, takes himself to be an expert on poetry, especially Homer's, becomes fodder for Plato's Socrates, who in comic fashion shows how little Ion knows. What is also revealed are Plato's views on poetry as a source of knowledge. Socrates explains to *Ion*, "It's not mastery that enables them [poets] to speak in those verses. . . . That's why the god takes their intellect away" (534 c).[2] The intellect and poetry are incompatible. "As long as a human being has his intellect in his possession he will always lack the power to make poetry" (534 b). A poet is unable "to make poetry until he has become inspired and goes out of his mind and his intellect is no longer in him" (534 b). Philosophy is an activity of the intellect, not so poetry. They are diametrically opposed.

Though Plato acknowledges that divine inspiration can have positive effects, he is wary of poetry for three interrelated reasons. First, poetry is full of falsehoods; its goal isn't truth. It is make-believe. Artists, literary or otherwise, merely imitate an appearance of reality, not reality itself. In Book X of the *Republic* (596e–598c), Plato illustrates what he has in mind with the example of a bed.[3] A real bed is perfectly a bed. It has all the characteristics a bed must have, and it has them without any particularities that a bed could lack. Think of a particular bed that a carpenter creates. It has some distinctive characteristics a bed does not need. Say it is eight feet long. Other particular beds are different lengths. So the carpenter's creation fails to be a bed in all respects and so fails to be a true bed. What is true of a bed cannot be gleaned from that example of a bed. It is only an appearance of a true bed, one way a bed can appear to us. Another appearance of a bed can differ from this one and still be a bed. Though they have something in common that makes them a bed, they differ in various ways. Suppose there were two perfect beds. There would still be one thing they had in common that makes them both beds and that would be the form of a bed, the perfect bed. So, there is only one true bed in reality, the form. All instances are simply appearances that are shadows of the form. If an artist paints a picture of a bed, such as Van Gogh's painting of his bed in Arles, it is only an imitation of an appearance of a particular bed. It shows that particular appearance from only one perspective and so fails to capture all the characteristics of that particular bed. It is only an imitation of that bed and doesn't represent that appearance in all its aspects. So it is farther removed from capturing the true bed. It is an imitation of a mere appearance of true reality. All art, poetry as well as painting, is this kind of imitation two steps removed from reality and cannot capture the truth about reality.

In Plato's Athens, the literary arts, including the great Greek dramas, were all poetry. But today the novel dominates contemporary literature. A novel by its nature is fiction, not a true narrative. The characters are not real people. The aim of fiction is not to tell a true story, a narrative of actual events that occurred in reality. The same was true of the drama and poetry of Plato's day, but his worry is more obvious now than ever. Every novel wears its fiction on its sleeve. To conceive of a work as a novel is to recognize it as fictional. Plato's second general concern is that poets, who depend for their creativity on divine inspiration, do not possess knowledge of the nature of things they write about. These days talk of divine madness seems, at best, a metaphor, and we might be tempted to dismiss this concern as a Platonic idiosyncrasy. That would be too hasty. His skepticism about poetry revealing knowledge of the nature of things is connected to his third, and most important reason, for rejecting poetry: knowledge involves understanding "the nature of things." To understand the nature of anything X we must be able to answer Socrates' question: what do all things X have in common that make them all X? But poetry cannot answer such Socratic questions. It lacks the appropriate method, what Plato dubs "dialectic." In the *Phaedrus*, Plato has Socrates explain why all writing falls short of dialectic:

> If anyone [including Homer and anyone else who has composed poetry] has composed these things with knowledge of the truth, if you can defend your writing when challenged with arguments, and if you can yourself make the argument that your writing is of little worth, then you must be called by a name not derived from these writings but rather from those things you are seriously pursuing (278c–d).[4]

The name of such a person is of course a lover of wisdom, a philosopher. Philosophy is done in speech, not writing. Margaret Atwood, reflecting on the nature of writers and writing, distinguishes between two manifestations of language in a passage Plato would have approved of:

> Writing had a hardness, a permanence, that speech did not. So as soon as tale-tellers took to writing—or as soon as other people took to writing down their tales . . . the writers-down became inscribers, and what they wrote took on a fixed and unchanging quality. God doesn't contend himself with speech or even with paper for the Ten Commandments: he chooses stone, thus emphasizing the solidity of what is written. Note however in the New Testament, Jesus is a tale-teller. He teaches by parable, but he doesn't write a word.[5]

The same can be said of Socrates as of Jesus, he did not write a word. For Plato, philosophy is best done by talking, not writing. Perhaps this provides the easiest, and most natural, explanation of why Plato wrote his philosophy in dramatic dialogue form. It is the best way in writing to capture how true philosophy is done.

Plato's criteria make it clear that philosophy is an activity of the intellect, not a matter of words. This is a standard that the poets, even Homer, cannot meet. Poetry, as well as other forms of fiction, is necessarily a matter of words. Yet, even if we set aside Plato's paradoxical condemnation of all writing, poetry and fiction—paradoxical since Plato himself wrote compelling dramatic dialogues and spun mythical tales as great as any literary artist—the fictive literary arts will still lack the necessary method for philosophy. Poetry and fiction do not provide arguments or reasons concerning the nature of things. Instead, at best, poetry and fiction focus only on particular instances. They take our attention away from reasons and the nature of things and direct it elsewhere, to mere distorted shadows of reality that fuel our passions. Only the intellect can comprehend reality, our senses afford us only these shadows, deceptive appearances of reality. Plato makes it clear in the *Phaedrus*, however, that instances of beauty can inspire us to contemplate the nature of beauty: "But now beauty alone has this privilege, to be the most clearly visible and the most loved" (250e).[6] The form of beauty—perfect beauty—is apparently closer to the senses because the characteristics of true beauty are most like the sensual in their effect on us. Plato plainly implies that in seeing an instance of beauty, one, especially one with a mature soul and control of one's passions, could be "moved to a vision of Beauty itself" (251a). Particular appearances of beauty that we grasp with our senses can, if we are not corrupted, cause us to contemplate beauty itself.

In modern fiction there is no place this idea is better explored than in Thomas Mann's *Death in Venice*, in which the main character, Gustav Auschenbach, himself a famous writer who, like Socrates in the *Phaedrus*, becomes smitten by the beauty of a boy. The boy's beauty has inspired the blocked writer to write again, and Auschenbach at one point tries to rationalize his obsession with the boy in these Platonic terms. When he sees the beautiful boy, this representation of beauty, he feels ecstatic, as though he has stepped out of himself into the realm of the forms. He believes he has grasped the form of beauty. "His eyes embraced the noble figure standing there at the edge of the blue, and in a rush of ecstasy he believed that his eyes gazed upon beauty itself, form as divine thought, the sole and pure perfection that dwells in the mind and whose human likeness and representation, lithe and lovely, was here displayed for veneration."[7] The experience causes him to feel free of constraints. "This was intoxication, and the aging artist welcomed it unquestioningly, indeed avidly. His mind was in a whirl, his cultural convictions in ferment; his memory cast upon ancient thoughts passed on to him in his youth though never yet animated by his own fire." Realizing that he is on the verge of losing control, Auschenbach raises a challenge to his Platonic revelry. Isn't this experience of sensual beauty—the beautiful boy—with the intoxication it brings, a threat to one's reason: "Was it not common knowledge that the sun diverts our attention from the intellectual to the sensual? It benumbs and bewitches both reason and memory such that the soul in its elation soon forgets its true nature and clings with rapt delight to fairest of sun-drenched objects." But having raised this question, he immediately gives a Platonic response, "Nay, only with the aid of the corporeal can it ascend to more lofty considerations." Then, much like Plato, Auschenbach provides a mythological example: "Cupid did as mathematicians do when they show concrete images of pure forms to incompetent pupils: he made the mental visible to us by using shape and coloration of human youths and turned them into memory's tool by adorning them with all the luster of beauty and kindling pain and hope in us at the sight of them." Unfortunately, Auschenbach seems to be his own counterexample.

Plato does believe that it is possible for the blessed soul and lover of wisdom to be inspired by sensual beauty to contemplate true beauty. However, he thinks for those who are not so blessed, their experience of beauty can have a different effect, as it ultimately does on Auschenbach in *Death in Venice*. Such beautiful appearances will fuel their passions to lead them astray: "If . . . they adopt a lower way of living, with ambition in place of philosophy, then pretty soon when they are careless because they have been drinking or for some other reason, [their] undisciplined horses will catch their souls off guard and together bring them to commit that act which ordinary people would take to be the happiest choice of all" (256c–d), and the result, Plato suggests, is a life of moral and spiritual corruption.[8] In *Death in Venice*, Mann portrays the degeneration and death of an artist, in particular a writer. Auschenbach, who is consumed by his experience of the beautiful boy—even though his desires are never acted upon or consummated—loses all control of his reason to his passions. Plato recognizes poetry's potential to inspire us to moral and spiritual knowledge, but he fears more the probability of its corrupting influence than the meager promise of its possible benefit. He believes more in the literary arts' power to fuel our irrational emotions than in their power to inspire us to understand the nature of things.

But even if poetry and fiction could, in the way Plato suggests, inspire us to inquire into the nature of things and so become philosophers, this contribution of poetry and literature would only be a *cause* of our doing philosophy. It would never be philosophy itself.

Recognizing the possibility of poetry to inspire us to philosophical reflection fails to relieve Plato's tension between philosophy and poetry or fiction in the least. The mere causal influence of poetry and fiction cannot provide any sense in which a literary work counts as seriously philosophical in a way that meets Plato's demands. It is difficult to see how it could. Suppose we acknowledge as philosophy proper any examination of how changes occur in our philosophical beliefs.[9] This move, Plato would suggest, is not best. It is fundamentally flawed since it asks us to commit the *genetic* fallacy, conflating reasons and causes, the origins of our beliefs, with the justification for our philosophical beliefs. All kinds of things can cause changes in our philosophical beliefs—the death of a parent or child, being imprisoned, having cancer, winning the lottery, just to name a few grand and melodramatic ones. These causes don't count as serious philosophy simply because they bring about a change in belief. The philosophical inquiry begins when we ask ourselves whether this change of belief is justified. For that matter, change of belief independent of the question of justification seems hardly relevant to what constitutes philosophy. Suppose someone never changed his or her philosophical beliefs; they are simply among the beliefs this person has always held. Such a person could still be a great philosopher because he or she has been dogged in subjecting those beliefs to scrutiny and searching for justification for them in the face of challenges. For Plato, change of beliefs seems an accidental psychological matter, not of the essence of what makes something philosophical, let alone what makes a literary text philosophical. This Platonic point is still with us. Frege, who insisted on it as strongly as Plato, puts it powerfully:

> Never, then, let us suppose the essence of the matter lies in such ideas. Never let us take a description of the origin of an idea for a definition, or an account of the mental and physical conditions on which we become conscious of a proposition for a proof of it. A proposition may be thought, and again, it may be true; let us never confuse the two things.[10]

To think that literature is philosophical because it changes beliefs, even our most basic ones, is a kind of psychologism.

So, Plato concludes in the *Republic*: "Poetry is not to be taken seriously or treated as a serious undertaking with some kind of hold on the truth, but that anyone who is anxious about the constitution within him must be careful when he hears it" (608a).[11] For Plato, most people's psychological makeup—the constitution within them—cannot be trusted not to succumb to poetry's irrational effects. The high likelihood of the devastating moral and spiritual costs are not worth the mere chance of intellectual gain. Plato thought it irrational to take this risk. So, he could not allow the poets in his republic. They had to go.

THE PERSISTENCE OF PLATO'S TENSION

You do not have to be Plato to feel the friction between philosophy and fictive literary arts. For Plato, philosophy is concerned with giving reasons, reasons for our most basic beliefs and assumptions that put the world together for us. Its goal is knowledge of one's self, the world, and society. Knowledge, however, presupposes truth and reason. From a false belief, we cannot gain knowledge of reality. False belief is dangerous. If you make a purchase for $1,500 believing that you have $2,000 in the bank when you only have $1,200, then you have undermined your own goals with the help of that false belief. To avoid this problem, we should strive for true beliefs. But a true belief is not enough for knowledge. You can have a true belief without knowing it is true. You could just be lucky to have arrived at that truth. Luck is not the best thing to count on as a guide to reality. So, Plato makes it clear that true belief alone falls short of knowledge. In the *Meno,* Socrates states what more is needed: true beliefs "are not worth much until one ties them down by (giving) an account of the reasons why."[12] Knowledge requires both truth and reasons. Each of these makes demands that fiction and poetry cannot meet. This realization is the legacy Plato bequeathed to all subsequent philosophers. It is very much still with us today.

That an unbridgeable gulf separates events and people in the real world from those depicted in fictive arts is a Platonic view reflected in the ideas of such contemporary philosophers as Gregory Currie and Kendall Walton.[13] Currie, in his book *Imagining and Knowing: The Shape of Fiction,* argues for the very Platonic thesis that fiction cannot teach us much, if anything, about people's thoughts, actions, desires, or emotions. The problem as he conceives it is that fiction does not lead us to beliefs. We imagine what is represented as happening in the fiction, and imagining is distinct from believing. It almost has to be. Belief aims at truth. Currie thinks this constrains what counts as belief: "In deciding whether a certain belief is the right belief to have, we should always ask how that belief stands to truth."[14] Imagining differs from belief in that respect. How things are in the world, the facts, do not constrain imagining. Imagining is only constrained by how things are represented in the fictional world, not the real world. The result is that we don't form beliefs when reading fictional literature. We only form quasi-beliefs. When we read a novel, say *The Great Gatsby*, we don't form the belief that Wilson killed Gatsby, but only a quasi-belief. What we might think of as our belief is only the imagining that Wilson killed Gatsby as represented in the fictional world of the novel. Neither do we feel any emotions nor have any desires, but only quasi-emotions and desires. We can't feel pity for Gatsby or wish he had ended up with Daisy. There is no Gatsby or Daisy for us to pity or wish for, only the Gatsby and Daisy as Fitzgerald created them in the novel. There is a lot that could be said about this view, and it deserves a thorough discussion, but suffice it to say here that this view of fiction puts it decidedly in Plato's camp.[15] Fiction doesn't lead to belief and so cannot lead us to true beliefs. Philosophy and fiction are thus as opposed as believing and imagining.

That knowledge requires reasons has had an even more pronounced influence on contemporary philosophy, one that still puts fiction and poetry at odds with the search for knowledge and reason is general. Thomas Nagel explains why: "The essential characteristic of reason is its generality. If I have reasons to conclude or to believe something or to want something, they cannot be reasons just for me—they would justify anyone else doing the same in my place."[16] The drive to understand with reasons—that understanding and reasons go hand in hand—demands a kind of abstract theorizing that ignores, and is at odds with, the unique details of concrete particulars that must be the focus in poetry and fiction. Theorizing about the world involves generalizing, abstracting, gleaning what is common to all things of a kind and ignoring the particular details that set them apart. Scientific theories lend understanding by using laws to explain unique and complex events, but they ignore the particular and idiosyncratic characteristics and conditions that set them apart. Hempel describes the classical, so-called 'covering-law' model of how this works:

> Every individual event, in the physical sciences no less than in psychology or the social sciences, is unique in the sense that it, with all its peculiar characteristics, does not repeat itself. Nevertheless, individual events may conform to, and thus be explainable by means of, general laws of the causal type. For all a causal law asserts is that any event of a specified kind, i.e., any event having certain specified characteristics, is accompanied by another event which in turn has certain specified characteristics; for example, that in any event involving friction, heat is developed.[17]

The covering-law model requires true laws. It requires true laws for real explanations. So, the demand for truth and the demand for reasons, with the abstraction and generalization that accompanies it, go hand in hand.

Truth and generalization can come apart. Not only logical positivists find compelling the idea that scientific theorizing and explanation involves abstracting from the infinitely detailed features that make any particular event unique. Such contemporary philosophers of science as Nancy Cartwright, who reject Hempel's so-called 'covering-law' model, emphasize the same point, with an albeit original twist, that scientific laws are abstractions and idealizations. They, Cartwright argues, are almost always *ceteris paribus* laws, true all things being equal. Since all conditions are never equal, they are true only in *ideal* circumstances, and so literally false about the detailed, complex features of the event in reality. For example, Galileo's First Law of Falling Bodies, that *in a vacuum*, all the freely falling bodies starting from rest cover an equal distance in an equal interval of time, 32 feet per second, or, in a vacuum all bodies starting from rest fall at the same rate. This is a *ceteris paribus* law. It is literally true only in ideal conditions, in a vacuum, and 'nature abhors a vacuum.'[18] There are no true vacuums in reality. Scientific laws explain, however, in virtue of this abstraction from, and idealization of, the concrete and unique details of the events they explain. She concludes that "most scientific explanations use *ceteris paribus* laws. These laws, read literally as descriptive statements, are false, not only false but deemed false even in the context of use. This is no surprise: we want laws that unify; but what happens may well be varied and diverse."[19] I will not take a stand on the controversial issue of whether scientific laws, in order to explain, must be true, or whether scientific realism or some form of instrumentalism is the best philosophical account. In either case, we are stuck with some picture of science explaining by abstracting from the particular concrete details of particular events, objects, and conditions. This picture is one we have all inherited from Plato.

Perhaps explanation and understanding need not always involve true belief or true laws. The need to generalize, idealize, and abstract remains. This Platonic demand still keeps poetry and fiction removed from the realm of knowledge and understanding. Think of a simple theoretical generalization in physics, $f = ma$, Force equals Mass times Acceleration. If this law is to explain the motion of all physical bodies, it is crucial that the general term "Mass" ignores the endless number of ways physical objects, and the conditions in which they exist, differ from each other. The theory does not care, because it finds unique details irrelevant, whether the object is a car of "rich cream color, bright with nickel, swollen here and there in its monstrous length with triumphant hatboxes and supper-boxes and tool-boxes, and terraced with a labyrinth of windows that mirrored a dozen suns,"[20] "that drove on toward death through the cooling twilight."[21] This disregard for detail in theorizing is not simply a matter of taste. It is essential to theoretical understanding that it ignore such details as much as it is to literature that it highlights them. The novelist Robert Owen Butler describes how this sensual detail is essential to the artistic success of a fiction writer: "Artists are not intellectuals. We are sensualists. The objects we create are sensual objects, and the way you'll know you're writing from your head is that you'll look at your story and find it is full of abstraction and generalization and summary and analysis and interpretation."[22] Writers of fiction and poetry avoid abstraction. It undermines their aesthetic success as literary artists. Scientific theorizing involves abstraction. Fiction, and poetry, demand rich detail that defies abstraction. The antagonism is real, not something Plato with his idiosyncratic political leanings made up. It was simply something he discovered. His tension seems as hard to avoid as it is to reconcile.

Any reasonable resolution of this conflict may seem to favor the methods of philosophy and science to fiction and poetry when it comes to the pursuit of knowledge and understanding. After all, even if we relax our strict concern for truth, reason's inherent demand for generalization and abstraction seems to force fiction and poetry out of the epistemic picture. The exclusion appears to be inescapable if knowledge is a species of belief and understanding in terms of reasons. Plato, like many philosophers since, ruled poetry and fiction out of the realm of knowledge and understanding. However, literary writers and artists often balk at this suggestion and advocate for the importance of fiction and poetry to understanding. If understanding human behavior is our goal, then many writers champion fiction and poetry over psychology. The acclaimed American novelist and short story writer Robert Boswell, who was a therapist before becoming a writer, explained in an interview with Terry Gross why he gave up psychology for fiction:

> [M]y interest in psychology and counseling stems from the same source as my interest in literature. I found that literature for me was a much more rewarding way to explore human behavior than psychology. I resist psychology more and more because it seems to me that any kind of ideology, adherence to any kind of ideology, places real limitations on your ability to understand humans and the world. It seems to me that psychology is the light that creates the darkness. That it may shine a very specific light on a very specific instance, but everything around it is dark. I'm less and less a believer in psychology.[23]

We should of course expect writers to favor their own craft, but many philosophers do not take such impressionistic talk seriously. They commonly think that novelists, poets, and other artists are not the best guides to *understanding* their art. Boswell uses the term "ideology" and the metaphor of the light and the darkness. Though it is not exactly clear what these terms mean for him, I think I can make sense of what it is that makes him skeptical of psychology and an advocate for fiction. The backstory he gives Gross offers a hint: "It really dawned on me when I was an undergraduate. I had been studying Freud in a class and then in a lit class I was reading Melville, and it seemed to me that Melville made a much more profound examination of the human experience than Freud."[24] Here is how I want to put what Boswell realizes. Freudian psychoanalysis may not be only an ideology in the pejorative sense of a set of ideas and beliefs that empower one class—the analysists—to control another—the patients. It is also an ideology in that it aspires to be a true scientific theory. Its goal is to explain all human behavior in terms of a few generalizations, the laws of psychoanalysis. Melville, the novelist, works in the opposite direction. He reveals an understanding of human behavior by focusing on the complexities in the concrete details of his characters' lives and the worlds they inhabit. The insight is in the complexity and detail. The abstractions and generalizations of a psychological theory may help us understand—cast light on—certain specific cases, but these are fairly exceptional. For most cases the resources of the theory miss the rich complexity necessary to lend any insight or understanding.

These claims are controversial to say the least. I will not only side with literature but defend a claim even more controversial. There are insights and understanding into human consciousness, behavior, and the world this consciousness moves in and through that psychology must miss. Indeed, any discursive theory will, whether scientific or philosophical in the traditional sense. The reason is that they cannot be put in words. They are unsayable, inexpressible in literal terms. They can only be shown. Some literary works of fiction and poetry depict them, show them to us. The result is a kind of knowledge, and *contra* Plato they play a crucial role in the philosophical project traditionally conceived. When fiction or poetry does this, it is philosophical. It does philosophy. The philosophy is in the showing not the saying. Sometimes it shows what cannot be said. I admitted this claim is controversial, but is the idea of the unsayable even coherent?

FICTION AND THE PARADOXICALLY UNSAYABLE

There is a tradition in philosophy that sees reason as paradoxically 'proving' its own limits, giving us reason to believe that there is something beyond reason. Of course, if there is, it is something that cannot be comprehended by reason—but of course it is reason showing us all this. Wittgenstein's *Tractatus* is a paradigm of this tradition. In it, he wanted to

> draw a limit to thinking, or rather—not to thinking, but to the expression of thoughts; for in order to be able to draw a limit to thought, we should have to find both sides of the limit thinkable (i.e. we should have to be able to think what cannot be thought.) It will therefore only be in language that the limit can be drawn.[25]

For Wittgenstein, the logic of our language shows this limit. Inherent in language is that it can point beyond itself to the unsayable. And paradoxically, it is what is unsayable that is the most important to Wittgenstein. Buddhist logicians, the greatest of which was Nagarjuna, reach similar conclusions. F. H. Bradley argued to the same end from different premises. The ultimate truth about reality could not be thought. It is ineffable.

Can some great literary works of fiction, poetry, and drama show or display something that cannot not be put literally into words—a world that can be understood only by revealing a reality that cannot be grasped in literal terms? Many writers often speak as if that is what they are doing. Consider how Stuart Dybek put it in an interview with Don Lee in *Ploughshares*:

> What's come to fascinate me more and more is trying to use language the way that the mediums of other arts—music in particular—are used, so that they lead you to nonverbal places. I don't know if it's a paradox or just foggy thinking to believe language can do the same thing, that language can in some way or another lead you to something unsayable.[26]

Paradoxical it may be, but I want to argue in the coming chapters that there may be nothing foggy about it. Literature, at its best, is finely focused on revealing, in the endlessly complicated details of life, a truth that cannot be articulated, only shown. The art is in selecting and arranging those details to reveal a truth that, ironically, transcends them yet resists statement in any generalization. The truth in fiction is not to be found in any theory. So much the better for philosophy and fiction. How is this possible? How can writers use words to say something that shows the unsayable? That is the immediate challenge I must face next.

NOTES

1. The scenario I imagine below is based on a particularly prevalent understanding of Plato that has been part of the philosophical lore since ancient times. I will not argue that it is correct or represents the true interpretation of Plato, since the details of any such historical argument are beyond the scope of this book. It does, however, represent an interpretation of first importance in the story of the tension between philosophy and the literary arts in the West.

2. Plato. *Ion*, in *Plato: Complete Works*, trans. Paul Woodruff, ed. John M. Cooper (Indianapolis: Hackett Publishing Company, Inc., 1997), 938–49.

3. Plato, *Republic*, in *Plato: Complete Works*, trans. G. M. A. Grube, rev. C. D. C. Reeve, ed. John M. Cooper, 972–1223.

4. Plato, *Phaedrus*, In *Plato: Complete Works*, trans. Alexander Nehemas and Paul Woodruff, ed. John M. Cooper, 507–56.

5. Margaret Atwood, *Negotiating the Dead: A Writer on Writing* (New York: Anchor Books, 2002), 47. Atwood does not mention or discuss Plato.

6. Plato, *Phaedrus*, 528.

7. All the quotes below from Auschenbach's description are taken from Thomas Mann, *Death in Venice*, trans. by Michael Henry Heim, introduction by Michael Cunningham (New York: HarperCollins, 2005), 80–81.

8. Plato, *Phaedrus*, 533.

9. One contemporary philosopher who proposes this idea is Philip Kitcher, who says, "A broader view of the activity of philosophizing, one in which what goes on in the mind of the subject can involve a range of different psychological processes—including experiments in imagination and emotional reactions to them—in which the texts and sounds that generate philosophical changes of mind can be far more various than the luminous rows of precise declarative sentences beloved by the popular model" (*Deaths in Venice* [Columbia University Press, 2013], 15).

10. Gottlob Frege, *The Foundations of Arithmetic*, trans. by J. L. Austin (Evanston, IL: Northwestern University Press, 1968), vi. I have no doubt that Kitcher is well aware of this passage.

11. Plato, *Republic*, In *Plato: Complete Works*, trans. G. M. A. Grube, rev. C. D. C. Reeve, ed. John M. Cooper, 1212.

12. Plato, *Meno*, in *Plato: Complete Works*, trans. G. M. A. Grube, ed. John M. Cooper, 871–97.

13. See Gregory Currie, *Imagining and Knowing: The Shape of Fiction* (New York: Oxford University Press, 2020), and Kendall L. Walton, *Mimesis as Make-Believe: On the Foundations of the Representational Arts* (Cambridge, MA: Harvard University Press, 1990).

14. Currie, *Imagining and Knowing*, 50. Currie's criterion doesn't commit him to saying that the aim of belief is truth.

15. Currie's view seems to have a bias in favor of the actual world. For modal realists, all worlds are equally real. If we can have beliefs about this world, there is no reason why we would not have real beliefs about other possible worlds, some of those being worlds of fiction. It seems to me this is a reasonable modal realist claim. I reserve attention to this interesting topic to another time.

16. Thomas Nagel, *The Last Word* (New York: Oxford University Press, 1997), 5.

17. Carl Hempel, "Studies in the Logic of Explanation." In *Introductory Readings in the Philosophy of Science*, 3rd edition, ed. E. D. Klemke et al. (New York: Prometheus Books, 1998), 212, 206–24.

18. This quip is usually attributed to Aristotle.

19. Nancy Cartwright, *How the Laws of Physics Lie* (Oxford: Oxford University Press, 1983), 52–53, 44–53.

20. F. Scott Fitzgerald, *The Great Gatsby* (New York: MacMillian, 1925), 68.

21. Ibid., 143.

22. Robert Owen Butler, *From Where You Dream: The Process of Writing Fiction*, ed. and with an introduction by Janet Burroway (New York: Grove Press, 2005), 14. Butler won the Pulitzer Prize for Fiction in 1993 for his book of short stories *A Good Scent from a Strange Mountain* (New York: Henry Holt, 1993).

23. "Writer Robert Boswell on Marriage and Divorce," interview by Terry Gross, *Fresh Air*, NPR, February 3, 1993, audio 16:25, https://freshairchive.org/segments/writer-robert-boswell-marriage-and-divorce.

24. Boswell recalls the same backstory in "You Must Change Your Life" (in *The Half-Known World: On Writing Fiction* [Saint Paul, MN: Graywolf Press, 2008], 175–85). There he says, "It was clear to me that Melville knew more about the human heart than Freud could dream of knowing" (180).

25. Ludwig Wittgenstein, *Tractatus Logico-Philosophicus,* 2nd edition, trans. D. F. Pears and B. F. McGuiness (London: Routledge & Kegan Paul, 1972, orig. 1922), 3.

26. Don Lee, "About Stuart Dybek," *Ploughshares* 24, no. 1 (Spring 1998): 192–98, 197.

Chapter 2

The Experience of the Unsayable

Saying the unsayable is an oxymoron. As soon as you hear the phrase, you know it is impossible, a contradiction. Any attempt is bound to fail. In David Foster Wallace's short story "Good Old Neon," the narrator, who seems to be speaking from the grave, repeatedly tries to describe what it is like to have your whole life flash before your eyes just before you die—"the internal head-speed or whatever of these ideas, memories, realizations, emotions"— only to end up frustrated. He explains that these thoughts "flash through your head so fast that *fast* isn't even the right word, they seem totally different from or outside of the regular sequential clock time we all live by, and they have so little relation to the linear, one-word-after-another-word English we all communicate with" that "deep down everybody knows it's [the attempt to convey it is] a charade."[1] Finally, he admits "the overarching paradox":

> [T]his whole thing where I'm saying words can't really do it and time doesn't really go in a straight line is something that you are hearing as words that you have to start listening to the first word then each successive word after that in chronological order to understand, so if I'm saying that words and sequential time have nothing to do with it you're wondering why we're sitting here in this car using words and taking up your precious time, meaning aren't I sort of contradicting myself right at the start.[2]

Philosophers have recognized a similar frustration, yet there remains a long history of philosophers who insist there are things that are unsayable. Kant famously began the *Critique of Pure Reason* with the idea: "Human reason has the peculiar fate in one species of its cognitions that it is burdened with questions which it cannot dismiss, since they are given to it as problems by the nature of reason itself, but which it also cannot answer, since they transcend every capacity of human reason."[3] F. H. Bradley argued from the nature of reason itself that "in the end Reality is inscrutable."[4] Wittgenstein put the idea in linguistic terms: "What we cannot think we cannot think; so what we cannot think we cannot *say* either."[5] Whatever answers there are cannot be thought, so they are not articulable. Wittgenstein concluded: "There are, indeed, things which cannot be put into words. *They make themselves manifest. They are what is mystical.*"[6] Are there things that are unsayable?

KANT ON THE LIMITS OF OUR KNOWLEDGE

A first thought might be that even to talk about things that are unsayable is already to say too much. If we are committed to there being a certain kind of object—those we can't talk about—we have characterized them as objects and thus said something positive about them. Kant struggled with this problem. His basic idea is that human knowledge is a product of the constitution of the mind and what the world outside the mind contributes to it. The nature of our minds sets limits on any possible knowledge. Knowledge of anything outside those limits is beyond us, unknowable. But to recognize this boundary is also to acknowledge that there is a way the world is in itself independent of the mind. This objective reality is unknowable by us, its true nature inconceivable to us. In his attempt to talk about this, Kant distinguishes what he called *phenomena* from *noumena*, things as they appear to us in contrast with things as they are in themselves:

> For if the senses merely represent something to us **as it appears**, then something must also be in itself a thing, and an object of non-sensible intuition, i.e., of the understanding, i.e., a cognition must be possible in which no sensibility is encountered, and which alone has absolutely objective reality, through which, namely, objects are represented to us **as they are**, in contrast to the empirical use of our understanding, in which things are cognized only *as* **they appear**.[7]

Kant makes it clear that there is no way for us to think about these objects. To think about an object is to group it under some concept, and we are limited to objects as they appear to us when we use our concepts. But then why insist that reality, as it is, consists of such noumenal *objects*? In what sense are they objects at all? Furthermore, in what sense is this noumenal reality one object or many? To talk of the noumenal as *objects* or things is to characterize them under the concept of *object* and thus to think about the unthinkable in a way that is contradictory. Kant's talk grants us too much. If we characterize the unsayable as objects or an object, then we have clearly said something about them.

Kant, of course, is not so clumsy. He makes two important points in his defense. First, the idea of a noumenal reality is not contradictory. The thought that there is a way reality is in itself that is different from the way it appears to us depends on the possibility that there is a kind of intuition or access to it that differs from ours. Given our limitation to the way things appear to us, we cannot have knowledge of the way reality is in itself. But there is nothing incoherent in the idea of beings with a different kind of cognitive ability, a kind of direct intuition of reality. Indeed, Kant thought God had that kind of immediate awareness of reality. There is no epistemic gap between God and reality in itself. Certainly, this is possible. Kant's second point is the idea of the noumenal as "only of negative use." He says it "limits the pretension of the sensibility." The idea limits our thought that reality must only be as it appears to us, "without being able to posit anything positive outside the domain of the latter."[8] Kant explains thus:

> Now in this way our understanding acquires a negative expansion, i.e., it is not limited by the sensibility, but rather limits it by calling things in themselves (not considered as appearances) **noumena**. But it also immediately sets boundaries for itself, not cognizing these things through categories, hence merely thinking them under the name of an unknown something.[9]

I find both of Kant's points suggestive. To avoid the quandaries Kant created with his objects or things in themselves, let's drop talk of the unsayable as a thing, an object, or objects. In fact, let's drop talk of *the* unsayable, with its definite article "the" that conjures up a unique thing or object. Instead, let's just say, negatively, that which is unsayable is something that cannot be said. This is not to attribute anything positive to that which is unsayable. It is simply to admit there is that which cannot be articulated, to admit there is a limit to what can be expressed in language. From this point on, I will use the expression "the unsayable" only as a *façon de parler* for that which is unsayable.

SENSE EXPERIENCE AND KNOWLEDGE BY ACQUAINTANCE

It seems Kant has shown us a way to talk about a limit to what is knowable and what is beyond those limits, if only in a negative sense. And we can name it, if we want, the unsayable, but with the assumption that this term only has a negative use. Though Kant set the limit at possible experience, there may well be inexpressible, unsayable aspects of reality within our experience as well. If we step back and take a break from the superstructure of Kant's baroque abstractions and take a hint from Wallace's short story, there are highly intuitive instances within our experience where language seems limited, where there is something missed in all articulations of the facts. Wallace's story is a wonderfully rich display of the perplexities and paradoxes of trying to understand or articulate the mental life of another person. First-person conscious experience is a prime candidate of something we have access to but that is inexpressible in words. Philosophers tend to focus on the sense of sight in most discussions of sense experience, but our other four senses provide similar cases of conscious experience that elude our ability to communicate what having that experience is like. Smell proves especially difficult to parse in any language approaching the literal. As Rachel Syme nicely puts is, "Smell—bodily and human yet invisible and heady—defies our expressive capacities in a way that other senses don't." She refers to "our clumsy efforts at the ineffable."[10] For example:

> Talking about smells can feel a little like talking about dreams—often tedious, rarely satisfying. The olfactory world is more private than we may think even when we share space, such as a particularly ripe subway car, one commuter may describe eau d'armpit as sweet Gorgonzola cheese, another will detect rotting pumpkin, and a third a barnyardy, cayenne tang.[11]

Syme's descriptions here show how we often use language to capture the experience of what we smell. She rightly notes that these attempts at describing what our experience is like are "a perfectly valid, even preferred way, to write about nasal experiences."[12] I would add that it might be the only way. Syme does not attempt to argue that smells are private and ineffable—that is not her purpose—but her examples of how we best attempt to put what it is like to smell something into words may provide a clue. Note first as she illustrates that we have a "perfectly valid" way to talk about these. We do it all the time. "Eau d'armpit" and "like sweet Gorgonzola cheese," though figurative and metaphorical, do describe the smell of the sweaty subway car. That is what the subway car smells like. But these descriptions do not reveal what it is like for you to have those experiences. Language still leaves us in the dark. William Lycan has made this distinction clear.[13] There are properties of our experiences that are describable—such as "smells like sweet Gorgonzola cheese"—and there is what it is like to experience them. The latter raises the question of ineffability. All we may be able to say is that "*it* makes me want to vomit." Description of what the smell is like, the phenomenal experience of the smell, defies us.

Add to that another aspect of smell that Syme points out. The nose brings to our consciousness many olfactory nuances "for which we rarely have a name."[14] I think this is an important, often overlooked detail about much of our psychological reality, and I will return to it later. For now, let's admit that we can coin a new term for an experience if we want. But it remains important that often we have no names for things as we experience them in our inner lives from our private points of view. Most of these have never had a name and never will.

At the end of her article, which returns to the personal tone with which it began, Syme concludes: "I have a new appreciation for the elusive quest to track down smells: while there is an undeniable appeal to pursuing a 'proper language' for discussing the osmocosm, there is also something to be gained by accepting that much of the pleasure of nasal perception is untranslatable."[15] I certainly concur. There is much to be gained in understanding how language, especially in some poems and fictions, shows us something about our conscious lives that cannot literally be said. It will also help us comprehend how poetry and fiction can direct us to knowledge that cannot be expressed. This domain of private, subjective experience is one of the places where the literary arts—plays, poems, fictions—can provide us knowledge that is literally unsayable in theoretical discourse.

Sense experience, as Syme's remarks about smell stress, is an obvious candidate of something we know but cannot express. But what is it exactly that we know yet can't express? A number of thought experiments have been created that may provide reasons not only that it is real but help explain why it is ineffable. One such scenario is Frank Jackson's case of "What Mary Didn't Know."[16] Mary is raised in a room where she is confined to a black-and-white world. All her experience of reality is black-and-white, without any color. But Mary is very well educated, so educated in fact, as Jackson puts it, that "she knows all the physical facts about us and our environment, in the wide sense of 'physical' which includes everything in *completed* physics, chemistry, and neurophysiology, and all there is to know about the causal and relational facts consequent on all this, including of course functional roles."[17] Yet given her complete knowledge of the physical facts, there is still something Mary doesn't know—she doesn't know what it is like to experience the color red, for example. When she does have the experience of red, she will have learned something.

Such cases as this are extremely controversial, and even if we take them as convincing, they don't show that what Mary knows is inexpressible in terms of facts stated in irreducible mental terms. That is, there could be expressible facts that are not physical facts. Let's grant Mary knowledge of all physical and mental *facts*. Give her all propositional knowledge in the 'wide' sense. Something Mary could know remains left out. To see how let's tweak Jackson's case. Make Mary blind. She doesn't grow up in a black-and-white world. She lives in a world without visual experience. Even if she has complete knowledge of all the physical and *mental* facts in the wide sense, there is something she will never know, that is, what it is like to experience red. All the talk in the world, all the expressible facts there are, will not bridge this gap for Mary. Conscious experience of color may well be best thought of as access to something inexpressible.

Let me suggest why I think knowledge of conscious experience, such as awareness of the color red, is a good candidate for knowledge of something that is unsayable. Philosophers usually think of knowledge as a kind of belief. A belief occurs when you accept a proposition as a fact—the way the world is—that F. Scott Fitzgerald is a novelist, that Baltimore is in New Jersey. Some beliefs are true, some false. But if all knowledge is a species of belief, then all knowledge will be propositional knowledge and will thus involve thought. To believe that Fitzgerald is a novelist you have to have that thought. To think that Fitzgerald is a novelist is to consider the object, Fitzgerald, under the concept *being a novelist*. Put simply, thinking is the ability to relate objects with concepts. If all knowledge is propositional, then all knowledge depends on thought, the ability to cut the world into categories with concepts.[18]

The point can be put more clearly in terms of language and sentences. To believe that Fitzgerald is a novelist is to assent to the truth of the sentence "Fitzgerald is a novelist." Sentences are made up of words related appropriately. The subject of the sentence is the proper name "Fitzgerald," the predicate is the phrase "is a novelist." The thought is that the predicate applies to the object so named. The sentence is true if the predicate applies to the object, false if it does not. True sentences reflect the way the world is, false ones do not. A belief is true when the sentence you assent to is true. Propositional knowledge is a species of true belief. Whether you think of knowledge in terms of propositions or sentences, it must depend on conceptual thought and language. So, if what Mary knows when she experiences the color red is propositional knowledge, it must be expressible, not unsayable.

All knowledge may not be propositional, however. It seems possible to have no knowledge of any truths about something at a time—as in Mary's case about the color red—but learn something about it by directly experiencing it, by being directly aware of it. What Mary learns is not based on any new awareness of facts about red but on her immediate experience of it. This kind of direct awareness is what Bertrand Russell dubbed *knowledge by acquaintance*: "We shall say we have *acquaintance* with anything of which we are directly aware, without the intermediary of any process of inference or any knowledge of truths." He added, "Knowledge of things, when it is the kind of knowledge we call *acquaintance*, is essentially simpler than any knowledge of truths, and is logically independent of any knowledge of truths."[19] It is difficult to believe that Mary needs to learn any more facts about red after her direct experience of it, if she is to know what it is like to experience the color red. Mary did come to know something new—what the experience of red is like—not by gaining new propositional knowledge but by her acquaintance with red. This acquaintance, as Earl Conee puts it, "requires the person to be familiar with the known entity in the most direct way possible for a person to be aware of a thing."[20] It may be expressible in propositional terms, now or at some time much later in the development of science. But Mary need not wait to learn something new. Her direct acquaintance with it suffices. She has learned something new as soon as she acquires this direct, non-propositional knowledge of it by acquaintance.

The same points about Mary's knowledge can be expressed in terms of subjective conceptions as opposed to an objective conception. Subjective conceptions depend essentially on a particular point of view. Objective conceptions characterize reality in terms that "can be observed and understood from many points of view and by individuals with different perceptual systems."[21] Thomas Nagel famously has us try to imagine what it is like to be a bat. Though we could know all the objective facts about bats, we cannot know what it is like to be a bat. Our imagination is restricted to our experience. So, try as I might to imagine what it is like to have bat experiences, experiencing the world as a bat, "I am restricted to the resources of my own mind."[22] There are subjective facts about bat reality that cannot be captured in objective terms. We cannot capture them in the literal terms of our language. They escape us. Nagel stresses: "The fact that we cannot expect to accommodate in our language a detailed description of . . . bat phenomenology should not lead us to dismiss as meaningless the claim that bats . . . have experiences fully comparable to in richness of detail as our own."[23] Bats know some things that can only be known by having experiences from their particular point of view. Likewise, Mary knows something that only she can know from her particular point of view. There is a subjective aspect of Mary's reality that cannot be captured in literal objective terms. Mary knows what her experiences are like because she has direct acquaintance with them.

Knowledge by acquaintance differs from propositional knowledge. Propositional knowledge is mediated by conceptual thought or language. Knowledge by acquaintance is unmediated by any concepts or language. It provides knowledge of reality that you will miss if you try to think of it in concepts or describe it in language. Knowledge by acquaintance is what is traditionally called "intuition," or in the religious case "revelation." Mystical revelation is knowledge of God based on direct awareness with the divine. It does not result in a set of truths or propositional knowledge about God.[24] In fact, this mystical revelation is always thought of as *ineffable*. It cannot be expressed in truths of language. To try to articulate it is, in the words of William James, "like translations of a text into another tongue."[25] What we are aware of in our direct acquaintance with our first-person states of consciousness may well be similarly ineffable, what we are aware of, unsayable. Religious mysticism aside, what we are immediately aware of in our first-person acquaintance with sensations seems to be a good, commonplace candidate for that which is unsayable.

PHILOSOPHY, POETRY, AND PERCEPTION

In his essay on Dante, T. S. Eliot focuses on how poetry can succeed as philosophy. Dante, Eliot says, deals with philosophy in his poetry better than any other poet.[26] Dante does not give us his philosophy in a theory but as something perceived. Poetry doesn't deal with ideas and arguments, at least if it's good poetry. It can, however, *manifest* these ideas. For Eliot, poets are not dealing with ideas but trying to realize these ideas. Poets don't argue for or against them, but present them as manifestations for inspection. Poetry becomes philosophy when it reveals or exhibits the ideas from the point of view of immediate experience.[27] I find this distinction very suggestive. Poetry, or literature in general, might show us something philosophical we can directly perceive, instead of theses, theories, or arguments we can say or articulate in sentences. Knowledge by acquaintance and first-person awareness of conscious states is a key that will help articulate this idea. The kind of knowledge we have of these states is direct or immediate in Russell's sense of knowledge by acquaintance—a kind of non-propositional *de re* relation between us and the objects of perception and introspection. If this is the case, then there are instances of knowledge that are not dependent on language. The knowledge is non-linguistic, more like what we commonly think of as intuition, or in religion, revelation. In the religious context, this kind of revelation is usually associated with mysticism. This connection between revelation and mysticism was not lost on Eliot who saw it as crucial to Dante's poetry. Dante did not contemplate the divine. He experienced it. His poetry did not try to excite the experience in us. It simply set the experience down for us, exhibited it.[28] Literature, at its best, sometimes makes such knowledge by acquaintance manifest and provides us with something analogous to revelation.

There may seem to be an obvious tension here. At least aspects of our conscious states are subjective. Cases like Mary's knowledge of what it is like to experience red and Nagel's attempt to imagine what it is like to be a bat highlight that subjectivity. These conscious states are essentially first-person. Objective reality is third-person; in Nagel's words, it can be "understood from many points of view." This sets up a dichotomy with what can be known only from a private, first-person point of view on the one side and what can be known from outside that point of view, from the third-person perspective, on the other. How can poetry bridge that gap better than any third-person description can? Dante may have set down and shown something he was directly acquainted with, but how can his poetry allow us to know what that experience was like for him? Several points need to be stressed before we address this issue. The poetry and fiction that shows the unsayable may or may not make us feel anything. As Eliot always insisted, the poet does not (and this should never be the poet's aim) try to excite emotions or other expressions in the reader. The poet, and I would say the fiction writer as well, tries to set these down, display them for us. Moreover, the writers, in the cases I have in mind, are not expressing their feelings. And if they do, that is not their goal. They are sharing their insight with us, revealing something about reality they are aware of or have been aware of immediately. The work shows it. The reader who engages the work can gain insight and understanding by recognizing and grasping what is shown.

My answer as to how this is possible and what exactly is going on here recalls Stanley Cavell's thoughts on skepticism and the problem of other minds.[29] Cavell is skeptical of the very problem. In a nutshell, the issue seems to be that I cannot know others exist because I cannot know their minds like I know mine. An epistemological gap separates us. The philosophical challenge is to provide rational grounds that will justify my belief in other minds. But even to recognize this problem or feel the force of it, Cavell thinks we must acknowledge others as separate from us. This acknowledgment is a presupposition of the problem and so cannot be questioned in any rational attempt to address the problem. My inability to know what your mind is like, what it is like from your point of view, is not an inability at all. It is inherent in that fact that you are a separate consciousness from me. If I could know your mind like I do my own, then I would cease to be me and you would cease to be you. Cavell illustrates this with a thought experiment.[30] Consider two brothers, First and Second. Second feels directly everything that First feels. If First is in pain, Second feels this immediately. Moreover, Second feels no pain unless First does. Any input to First's senses that gives rise to an immediate experience in his consciousness is immediately and directly experienced by Second. If First feels nothing, Second likewise feels nothing. If we generalize this to all of Second's immediate experience, the conclusion seems to be that, as Cavell says, "while we still have pain in two bodies, we no longer have so to speak, two *owners* of pain."[31] What the example does is obliterate any distinction in the subjective states of the two bodies that would give us two separate conscious beings. In order to state the problem of other minds we must first acknowledge the inherent separateness of subjective states. We must acknowledge others. So, for Cavell, acknowledgment precedes any rational reflection about them. It is a kind of metaphysical postulate presupposed by the very debate.

I will not take a stand on skepticism or whether Cavell has sufficiently handled it. But I think his terminology and distinctions here are relevant to articulating how poetry and fiction can show the unsayable. If someone is expressing a first-person subjective state, either through language or other behavior, Cavell says that person is *exhibiting* that state. I do not experience that first-person state. I cannot have your conscious experience. But I can recognize it either as one I have immediate awareness of or am vaguely aware of. When I do this, I come to experience several insights. First, I can gain a heightened awareness of a state of consciousness never recognized before or only vaguely so. Second, I acknowledge you as other than me, a separate consciousness, with a range of possible thoughts and feelings such acknowledgment brings in its wake. I want to suggest that some works of fiction and poetry exhibit some such first-person states of consciousness that are inexpressible. I also want to point out that this way of looking at how knowledge by acquaintance works in some literary works avoids any worries of the kind Currie raises for such accounts. For him fiction cannot acquaint us with any feelings such as empathy for the characters. I cannot empathize with Gatsby in his feelings for Daisy. There is no Gatsby and there are no such feelings with which I can empathize. In my view, we need not have feelings for the characters. Instead, we recognize feelings we are acquainted with that the work exhibits. These works display states that, as Nagel says, "we cannot expect to accommodate in our language a detailed description of."[32] They are unsayable.

IS SENSE EXPERIENCE INEFFABLE BY DEFINITION?

Some philosophers may agree that our knowledge of what it is like to have an experience, say of red, is non-propositional and ineffable. They may nonetheless find these cases uninteresting. An aspect of sense perception may be inexpressible but only in a trivial sense.[33] If sense perceptions are ineffable *by definition*, then they may not present an interesting case of something unsayable. I will take up the distinction between the trivial ineffable and the philosophically interesting, in principle ineffable in the next chapter. Here I want to consider the claim that what we are directly acquainted with in sense perception or experience is ineffable by definition. That phenomenology of sense experience is ineffable should be, on this view, unsurprising due to the fact that it is inexpressible by definition. Just as it is unsurprising and unenlightening to be told that every bachelor is unmarried or a U.S. citizen is a recognized member of the nation, it should be equally uninteresting that a sense experience is ineffable. To understand the terms "bachelor," "U.S. citizen," and "sense experience" is to know these statements are true.

This aspect of sense experiences—the qualia or raw feels—is precisely what I believe is one of the things we have knowledge of by direct acquaintance. Is this aspect of experience ineffable by definition? My worry concerning this claim is what definition of first-person experience would have this result? Few acceptable definitions come to mind that would make the phenomenal aspect of experience inexpressible by definition. Consider, for example, a following first shot at a possible contender, where φ is a verb for one of the five senses—see, taste, smell, hear, touch—and x is the object of that verb.

1. What it is like to have the experience of φ-ing $x =_{def}$ a private, first-person state of consciousness that occurs upon or while φ-ing x.

A typical instance of this would be what it is like to have the experience of tasting Hagen Das chocolate ice cream. It is a private, first-person state of consciousness that occurs while tasting Hagen Das chocolate ice cream. It is known by direct acquaintance in Conee's sense and is subjective in Nagel's. Does this definition suffice to make the experience ineffable by definition? Not yet. An experience could meet the definition, that is, be a private, first-person state of consciousness that occurs upon or while having that experience, but only accidentally, so to speak, by happenstance. It might, for all the definition demands, be a private, first-person state that could, in some possible world, perhaps even this one, be translated into third-person terms. In other words, it would be expressible. This difficulty is in no way avoided if we agree that the definition itself is necessary:

2. Necessarily, what it is like to have the experience of φ-ing $x =_{def}$ a private, first-person state of consciousness that occurs upon or while φ-ing x.

Let this be the case. So, that the definitional relationship holds in all possible worlds. Still, in each of these worlds it remains possible that, for all the definition demands, there is a theory that explains and translates this private, first-person aspect of experience into third-person terms.

This does not mean that the theory providing the translation and explanation be available in the actual world where the experience occurs. It only amounts to there being a world accessible from the world where the experience occurs in which such an objective, third-person theory is available. So, any definition that implies that this aspect of experience is inexpressible must be stronger. For each world in which the experience occurs we might suggest adding the wrinkle that these properties be essential. What it is like to have an experience of something is *essentially* private and *essentially* first-person:

3. Necessarily, what it is like to have the experience of φ-ing $x =_{def}$ an essentially private, essentially first-person state of consciousness that occurs upon or while φ-ing x.

This seems a necessary addition if we are to make this aspect of experience inexpressible by definition, but by the same token, it has now become more contentious. Much of the debate over the nature of qualia and our knowledge of them centers on exactly the question of whether qualia and our knowledge of them can be captured in or reduced to terms of a scientific theory which is objectively public and shareable. This stronger definition begs that very question. The issue over qualia is whether all properties of qualia can be rendered in objective terms. To insist that qualia are essentially private by definition is to ignore and make meaningless any controversy to the contrary. It presupposes an answer to the question at issue. It cannot provide an answer to it.

You may want to continue to search for a definition that avoids these pitfalls, but I have serious general concerns about establishing a substantial, especially non-controversial, solution to this philosophical issue by appeal to definition. Our most plausible contenders for definitions are only as good as our overall current knowledge and the language that expresses it. What once seemed inconceivable 'by definition' often becomes true in later, richer theories. What was inconceivable and inexpressible by definition becomes not only literally expressible but true. For example, it was once thought true by definition that if two objects were falling, then they must both be going in the same direction. At that time, it would have been inconceivable, and likewise inexpressible, that two objects could be falling but in opposite directions. It may have been put into words, but any such statements would have been incoherent in the language at hand. Any attempt to state it would have been a contradiction and as inconceivable as an inconsistent state of affairs. The assumption behind the definition was that the earth was flat, not a sphere. The definition was only as good as the overall view of the world it was based on. We know now that the world is roughly spherical. It is not only expressible but true that two objects can fall in opposite directions. It happens all the time. It will not do to insist that our language, with its definitions, is simply much better than the earlier one. The evolution of our language was of a piece with the overall growth of knowledge. As Quine taught us, "It is nonsense, and the root of much nonsense, to speak of a linguistic component and a factual component in the truth of any individual statement."[34] Whether as a matter of fact qualia can be rendered in objective terms cannot be answered by stipulating a definition. Our best definitions reflect our current theories and are revised as we acquire new knowledge. This is why any attempt to define sense experience in such a way as to make it inexpressible by definition is bound to be inconclusive.

For my part, I do believe that we each have direct knowledge by acquaintance of what it is like to have our own sense experiences. I will not venture to guess whether that knowledge will someday be expressible in the objectively shareable propositions of a plausible theory. The problem may be a hard conceptual nut to crack. There are reasons for thinking it is unlikely, if not impossible. It may be in knowledge and language far beyond our wildest imagination. I do not know how to determine the issue either way in advance. What I will argue in the next chapter, however, is that even though perhaps temporary, the currently inexpressible nature of what we know by direct acquaintance is not philosophically trivial. There remains a philosophically significant sense in which, at least for now, we know something unsayable that can only be shown, not said.

NOTES

1. David Foster Wallace, "Good Old Neon," *Oblivion: Stories* (New York: Little Brown and Company, 2004), 141–81. All the pieced-together quotes are from page 151.

2. Ibid., 152.

3. Immanuel Kant, *Critique of Pure Reason*, trans. and ed. Paul Guyer and Allen W. Wood (Cambridge University Press, 1997), 99, A vii. First published in the A edition 1781, then revised as the B edition in 1787. This passage only occurs in the first edition.

4. F. H. Bradley, *Appearance and Reality* (Oxford University Press, 1893).

5. Ludwig Wittgenstein, *Tractatus Logico-Philosophicus*, 2nd edition, trans. D. F. Pears and B. F. McGuiness (London: Routledge & Kegan Paul, 1972, orig. 1922), 5.61, 115.

6. Ibid, 6.522, 151.

7. Kant, *Critique of Pure Reason*, 347, A 249–50. In this translation, the bold in italics appear there in bold print. The emphasis is in the original.

8. Ibid., 350, A 255, B 311.

9. Ibid., 351, A 256, B 312.

10. Rachel Syme, "On the Nose: How to Make Sense of Smells," *New Yorker*, February 1, 2021, 5.

11. Ibid.

12. Ibid.

13. William Lycan, *Consciousness and Experience* (Cambridge, MA: M.I.T. Press, 1996), 91–108.

14. Ibid., 58.

15. Syme, Ibid., 60.

16. Frank Jackson, "What Mary Didn't Know," *The Journal of Philosophy* 83, no. 5 (May 1986): 291–95. Jackson's point is not to argue for the unsayable or inexpressible

nature of mental experience but only to argue that physicalism is false. But I find these cases at least suggestive of the possibility of something inexpressible.

17. Ibid., 291.

18. I realize there are other, broader, uses of the word 'thought.' I will restrict the term here to what we might instead call 'conceptual thought,' though I find the qualification redundant. But I will sometimes add the modifier to make clear what I intend by thought or thinking.

19. Bertrand Russell, *The Problems of Philosophy* (Oxford University Press, 1912), 46. He adds to the above passage, "It would be rash to assume that human beings ever, in fact, have acquaintance with things without knowing some truth about them."

20. Earl Conee, "Phenomenal Knowledge," *Australasian Journal of Philosophy* 72, no. 2 (1994): 136–50, 144.

21. Thomas Nagel, "What It Is Like to Be a Bat," *The Philosophical Review* 83, no. 4 (October 1974): 435–50, 442.

22. Ibid., 439.

23. Ibid., 440.

24. Lao Tzu seems to express the idea that the Tao cannot be captured in words: "The way [the Tao] is forever nameless." Words cut reality into bits that limit it and always leave something unsaid: "Only when it [the Tao] is cut are there names" Lao Tzu, *Tao Te Ching*, trans. D. C. Lau (New York: Penguin Books, 1963), Book 1, Ch. XXXII, 72, 91.

25. William James, *Varieties of Religious Experience* (London: Longmans, Green, 1905), 431.

26. T. S. Eliot, "Dante," *The Sacred Wood* (London: Methuen & Co., Ltd, 1920), 170–71.

27. Ibid., 162–63.

28. Ibid., 170. I have much to say about Dante and Eliot and how poets can do philosophy with poetry in chapter 5.

29. Stanley Cavell, "Knowing and Acknowledging" in *Must We Mean What We Say*, updated edition, (Cambridge, UK: Cambridge University Press, 2002), 220–45.

30. Ibid., 232–33.

31. Ibid., 232.

32. Nagel, "What It Is Like to Be a Bat," 439.

33. Silvia Jonas, *Ineffability and Its Metaphysics*, (Palgrave Macmillan, 2016), 6. Below I am thinking primarily of her argument to this conclusion.

34. W. V. Quine, "Two Dogmas of Empiricism," in *From a Logical Point of View*, 2nd edition, revised (Cambridge, MA.: Harvard University Press, 1980), 42.

Chapter 3

The In Principle Ineffable and the Trivially Ineffable

Kant, Bradley, and Wittgenstein all thought of the unsayable as ineffable *in principle*. The idea prevails that this is the only way the unsayable matters. W. E. Kennick flatly asserts, "Only the ineffable in principle is of philosophical interest."[1] It is telling that he provides no reasons for this claim, as though it goes without saying. What it means to say that something is ineffable *in principle* is usually stated as casually as Kennick does: "that for which there are and can be no suitable words, that for the expression of which all possible words are unsuitable."[2] But the devil is in the modal modifiers. "Can" in what sense? "Possible" for whom? How we answer these questions matters to the philosophical importance of the unsayable. The subtleties involved are as surprising as their significance.

A close look into a recent attempt to distinguish the philosophically interesting in principle ineffable from the trivially ineffable will prove highly instructive.[3] Silvia Jonas considers three kinds of examples of the ineffable that she rejects in turn as trivial and so philosophically uninteresting. First, there are things inexpressible due to *nescience*, "not ineffable *in principle*, but only for subjects with specific epistemic constraints."[4] For example there are things that cannot be expressed at a particular place or time: "names for animals or diseases that haven't been discovered yet, names of historical events lying in the future, names of people from the distant past, etc."[5] Being born at a particular time limits our knowledge. In these cases, the lack of knowledge can in principle be overcome. Someday people will know and express things we have no inkling of now. This kind of ineffability is alleged to be of suspect philosophical interest. The inexpressibility in these cases "is a consequence of their [the inexpressible things'] extrinsic properties, that is, of the way in which the subjects in question are related to the respective entities."[6]

Similar things can be said about a second class of cases, those where the ineffability is due to physical constraints. Most, if not all, things will be inexpressible to a person who is gagged. This contingency is obviously a case of something that is only *in practice* ineffable. A gag can easily be removed. A more interesting case of a physical constraint is being finite. A finite being cannot express an infinite proposition "using finite resources in a finite amount of time."[7] For a different example, Jonas has us imagine Lew and Keith. We recognize and distinguish them by their faces. We know one from the other. Yet it may be "impossible to express our knowledge that this is Lew's rather than Keith's face," due to the fact that we are unable consciously to discriminate all the details that distinguish their faces. In this case, "the abundance of detail overcharges our conceptual resources."[8] On the face of it, this example seems to be ineffable due to nescience, not physical constraints. Even though it may be due to limitations of our physical makeup, the problem is with our ability to express in scientific terms what we know. It is conceivable that this knowledge is expressible in a richer theory. Our conceptual limitations are the problem, not any physical constraints.

The last purported class of examples of the trivially inexpressible involves category mistakes. Take a stone.[9] Stones are not the kind of thing that could be expressible, so stones are ineffable, but only trivially so. This example is odd. It is hard to believe anyone thinking a stone could be expressible. The example is extreme, but that is the point. The category mistake is as drastic and crazy as thinking the number 1,435 is purple. By analogy, numbers cannot have colors, but it is trivial that they are colorless. More interesting is Jonas' claim that sense perceptions are unsayable in the same trivial way. Like stones, sense perceptions are not the kind of things that can be expressed at all: "It is impossible to express the sense perception of tasting saffron *in such a way that another person will come to know how saffron tastes.*"[10] Jonas claims that sense perceptions are inexpressible by definition, and so, as with objects like stones, logically impossible to express.[11] As I have argued in chapter 2, that is dubious, but let's here suppose it is true for the sake of the distinction between the trivially inexpressible and the interestingly ineffable in principle.

Questions about the case of sense perceptions aside, when we turn our attention to reputed in principle cases, a sharp distinction between those and the trivial ones becomes difficult to draw. Consider Jonas' first case of the interestingly ineffable—aspects of some works of art: "Many would agree that it is impossible to express the meaning of a painting, a melody, or a poem in literal language without remainder."[12] This claim is almost certainly true, but the exact claim is true of sense perceptions as well. Most would agree that it is impossible to express the taste of a particular wine in literal language without remainder. So, this appeal to popular opinion—what most people would agree to—provides no reason to separate the interesting from the trivial cases of in principle inexpressibility.[13]

A significant difference may lie in the thought that works of art have a 'meaning' that is not expressible in literal language. But what is meant by 'meaning' here? Surely not anything like propositional meaning. Consider a proposed argument: "If there were no substantial difference between meaning that can be transported through literal language and meaning that can be conveyed through works of art, art would be pointless."[14] A simple *modus tollens* syllogism renders the crucial claims clear. I state the premises in the indicative mood.

1. If there is not a substantial difference between meaning that can be transported through literal language and meaning that can be conveyed through works of art, then art is pointless.
2. Art is not pointless.
3. So, there is a substantial difference between meaning that can be transported through literal language and meaning that can be conveyed through works of art.

Defending either premise presents difficulties. Though artworks may sometimes express some things much better than what can be expressed by other means, this fact alone does not make what it 'means' inexpressible in principle. Yet it would be enough to justify that creating art is not pointless—since art is able to express better what other means of expression cannot. The second premise—that art is not pointless—in some sense almost goes without saying, but it likewise raises hard questions. In a trivial sense, art is not pointless in that there are many reasons for doing art: the enjoyment it gives people—the people who enjoy creating and sharing it as well as those who experience it; the purpose it brings to the artists' lives; the various impacts and significance it has on society. The list could go on.

My point is that the second premise of the argument is easily true in many ways that don't depend on any claims about whether works of art have a meaning that is inexpressible in principle in literal language. In order for the argument to be telling, there must be a connection between the sense of 'pointless' in the consequent of the first premise and the claims about meaning in the antecedent. This takes us back to the question of what it means to say a work of art has a 'meaning' that is non-propositional and cannot be put in literal terms without leaving something unsaid. A dilemma looms here. Either the sense of 'meaning' conveyed by works of art is semantic or it is not. If it is semantic, then it is possible to put it into linguistic terms without remainder. If it is not semantic, then the challenge is to explain what that sense is without appeal to its significance in our lives or what the experience of it is like. Jonas' explanation seems to suggest that the meaning is in the experience: "It is experienced by almost everyone at some point in their lives. Sooner or later, everybody is confronted with a piece of art, or an aesthetically gripping natural scene, which seizes them and reveals something to them that they cannot express."[15] Aside from committing the fallacy *ad populum*, the claim makes matters worse for the distinction between the trivially and interestingly ineffable in principle. On the face of it, the statement is most certainly false. I doubt whether most people in the population ever have such aesthetic experiences. Many people may, but how many people do not? Given the conditions of many people on the planet it seems likely that such aesthetic experiences are precious. That of course does not make them unimportant to this debate, but the numbers may not matter. What is worse is that even if this claim is true of an important limited number of people, it tells against Jonas' distinction, not in favor of it. The confrontation with the art is said to reveal something to them that they cannot put into words. The problem is that many people are unable to put many things into words because they are not articulate or educated enough. So, the fact that they cannot put things into words is no reason to believe that such experiences are in principle inexpressible. Is this inexpressibility a reflection of people's linguistic limitations or is it intrinsic to the aesthetic experience? At this point, the line between trivially inexpressible and the interestingly in principle inexpressible blurs.

Perhaps a wedge may be driven between the trivial inexpressibility of sense experiences and the interesting cases with religious experiences or religious knowledge—the most widely recognized contender for the ineffable in principle. Of religious knowledge, Jonas says: "It is almost tautological to say that it is impossible to express one's knowledge of God in such a way that someone else comes to know that God exists."[16] This is a strange claim, given that according to Anselm, it is almost tautological—based on the definition of God—that it is not only possible, but doable to express knowledge of God in such a way that someone else—"the fool [who] hath said in his heart: there is no God"—comes to know that God exists.[17] That is the whole point of the ontological argument for the existence of God. The ontological argument may ultimately fail, but that the argument in the tradition of Leibniz, Gödel, Hartshorne, and Plantinga is still a much-discussed contender in the philosophical debate is enough to show that it is not impossible by definition.[18] I have my doubts about the success of these arguments, but certainly not because they are logically incoherent. If there is no God, it will be impossible to express any claims such that someone else comes to know of God's existence. But that seems certainly a case of trivial ineffability, if ever there was one, since the same can be said of expressions that would bring anyone to know of the existence of anything that doesn't exist.

Religious knowledge based on religious experience may provide the strongest case for the ineffable in principle: "It is impossible to express other religious experiences, for example the oneness of everything there is, in such a way that enables another person to have the same experience."[19] Focus on religious experience takes us back to the nature of sense experiences in general, which are supposedly trivially ineffable. Shouldn't this make religious experiences trivially ineffable? Jonas admits that there is an aspect of religious experience that, like any other experience, is trivially ineffable. What it is like to have the religious experience is trivially ineffable by definition. Yet religious experiences apparently have "an additional ineffable aspect."[20] Religious experiences cannot be intentionally invoked, she claims, though ordinary experiences can. If I want you to experience what my wine tastes like, I can simply pass you my glass, but "there is no obvious way" I can invoke my religious experiences in you.[21] Also, Jonas finds it important to religious experiences that not everyone can have them. These features give religious experiences a non-trivial ineffability that ordinary sense experiences lack.[22]

On the contrary, fairly obvious ways exist to invoke one's religious experiences in others just as they do ordinary experiences. There are standard religious practices and disciplines—prayer, meditation, yoga, fasting—that one can be taught to invoke religious experiences. These religious practices and disciplines may take time to master, but they can be taught and they can result in common religious experiences. This kind of religious training is no different in kind from training to become a sommelier. Moreover, some religions invoke shared religious experiences through the use of drugs, such as peyote in Native American religions. Timothy Leary championed LSD to 'turn on' a generation to experience God. That isn't significantly different from me sharing my wine to invoke in you the experience of the taste of my wine. True, not everyone can have religious experiences, but the same can be said of ordinary experiences. If you are colorblind, I cannot, try as I might, invoke in you the experience of red. With all the training in the world, some people could never develop the taste of a sommelier. People who cannot have religious experiences may have similar perceptual limitations. These limitations, like other cognitive limitations Jonas mentions, seem to be in practice, not in principle, constraints. Religious experiences may be of special interest because of the importance of their content, but this feature doesn't give us any reason to believe they are especially different in kind from ordinary experiences *qua* experiences.

I have belabored these points in order to emphasize just how difficult it is to characterize what it means to be 'in principle' ineffable and to draw attention to the challenges of drawing a sharp line between the in principle ineffable and the trivially ineffable. One way to address this problem in a general way would be to provide a transcendental argument that some things must be inexpressible. Philosophers like Kant, Bradley, and Wittgenstein seem to suggest such transcendental arguments for ineffability or unknowability. A successful transcendental argument is a tall order. A transcendental argument that justifies and explains a category of in principle unsayable things may be possible. But I want to suggest that we may not have to wait on one to arrive on the philosophical scene in order to understand the significance of the unsayable, especially in the literary arts. There are some cases of inexpressibility that are clearly uninteresting, such as being gagged. But there may be many cases of ineffability that are due to our cognitive and physical limitations, as well as other contingencies, that are nonetheless deeply interesting and significant cases of ineffability. The question of whether they are unsayable in principle or not may be moot. Philosophers' insistence that only the in principle ineffable is of philosophical interest may be misguided.

LANGUAGE, LANGUAGES, AND THE UNSAYABLE

A simple, almost natural, definition of the inexpressible in principle may seem obvious: that which not even God could express. If God is omniscient and omnipotent and God cannot express it, it is not expressible. This definition is attractive in its simplicity. It seems impossible to dispute. Try thinking of a counterexample. Any proposed case would only show the poverty of one's conception of God. Moreover, this definition does not make the ineffable depend on any contingent limitations that could be eliminated. God doesn't have any. This definition definitely draws a sharp line, but also makes quick work of the topic. There is nothing inexpressible by God, so there is nothing inexpressible in principle. The philosophical baby gets thrown out with the omniscient bathwater.

Since the issue of ineffability, inexpressibility, or the unsayable involves essentially a linguistic limitation, it forces us to think carefully about the nature of language and languages, even if we are going to bring God back into the picture. Consider again the case of what Mary did not know and her new experience of red. I suggested she comes to have new knowledge of red through direct, non-propositional acquaintance. But is what Mary knows when she is aware of red really inexpressible? After all, we do have words in the language—"red," "color," "sensation"—for what she is acquainted with. With the appropriate vocabulary it seems that what we are directly acquainted with in sense experience would become propositional knowledge after all. This way of considering what Mary comes to know could be taken to suggest that whether something is unsayable or not depends on how rich the language is. If that is the case, then there won't be anything that is unsayable in principle, but only relative to a given language. It almost goes without saying that there are things inexpressible in some languages. Consider the blocks language that Wittgenstein describes in the opening of the *Investigations*:

The language is meant to serve for communication between a builder A and an assistant B. A is building with building stones: there are blocks, pillars, slabs and beams. B has to pass the stones, and in the order in which A needs them. For this purpose, they use a language consisting of the words 'block,' 'pillar,' 'slab,' 'beam.' A calls out;—B brings the stone which he has learnt to bring at such-and-such a call.—Consider this as a complete primitive language.[23]

Practically anything we say on a daily basis is unsayable in that language. In that language, I can express my desire for you to bring me a slab, but not an ice cream cone. There simply is no word for ice cream cone in that language. Considering cases like Wittgenstein's inspires philosophers to conclude that the unsayable is only philosophically interesting if it is inexpressible *in principle*, not as an accident of the poverty of a particular language. If what is unsayable in one language can be expressed in a richer language, then there is nothing unsayable in reality but only relative to some language or other.

Recall from chapter 2 the William James quote in which he likens the ineffable to translating into another tongue. The issue of the unsayable can be put in terms of translation. James' suggestion seems to be: what is ineffable or unsayable is not capable of being translated or rendered into another language, no matter how rich. Of course, the analogy of translation is imperfect. Translation is a relation between distinct languages. That which is unsayable is not expressible in a language to be translated. But James' analogy remains suggestive—any attempt at translation will, in principle, leave something out since it simply cannot be said. There will be no common measure for the unsayable in any possible language. Even God, with omniscient knowledge of all possible languages, could not render it into words without loss.

Mark Walker, taking a lead from what Donald Davidson calls "the flexibility and expandability of natural languages," puts the issue in terms of *semantic expansion*.[24] If the semantic limitations of a language make some things unsayable, the crucial question is whether that language could be semantically enriched so that what was once unsayable becomes perfectly expressible. If so, then what was once unsayable is no longer unsayable. If semantic expansion of a language is always possible, then there is nothing in principle unsayable. Semantic expansion basically occurs when the resources of a richer language are used to expand the more primitive language by adding new means of expression to the latter. As Davidson says there is no reason for "this to require word-by-word translation."[25] It may take many sentences as well as extra-linguistic learning to add a new word to the vocabulary of the impoverished language and make an idea that was formerly unsayable expressible.

Walker provides a simple argument, following Davidson, that semantic expansion is always possible. Take any two languages L_1 and L_2. Let L_2

be the semantically richer language. L_2 can express things unsayable in L_1. Expand L_1 to include all of L_2. This new language, the union of L_1 and L_2, can now express anything in L_1 and L_2. Imagine this process continuing to include all natural languages. Walker says, "Any particular language might evolve into THE LANGUAGE—the union of all natural languages ($L_1 + L_2 + L_3 \ldots$) through semantic expansion. In other words, THE LANGUAGE contains all natural languages as subsets of itself."[26] Whatever is expressible is expressible in THE LANGUAGE. Of course, this doesn't quite take us to the conclusion that there is nothing unsayable in THE LANGUAGE. At a given time, there could be something unsayable even in THE LANGUAGE. However, as Walker insists, there is no reason why THE LANGUAGE, at any given time, cannot itself be semantically expanded with the growth of knowledge and the coining of new terms so that THE LANGUAGE$_1$ semantically expands into THE LANGUAGE$_2$. This process can be repeated just as before with the natural languages, taking the union of THE LANGUAGE$_1$ and THE LANGUAGE$_2$ to expand into a new language THE LANGUAGE$_3$ and so on *ad infinitum*. The idea is reminiscent of Tarski's infinite hierarchy of formal languages which has each metalanguage containing the one below it.[27] Walker is proposing the possibility of something akin to this for natural languages. Of course, if Davidson's semantics for natural languages is correct and Tarski's truth definition for a language provides any adequate account of meaning in a language, then Walker's idea of an infinite semantic expansion of the language will amount to Tarski's infinite hierarchy of formal languages. In any case, anything unsayable in THE LANGUAGE at any given time will be swallowed up in the swell of this semantic expansion, so that nothing is left unsayable in principle. If this is the case there is nothing unsayable in a philosophically interesting sense.

This argument for semantic expansion takes us to the heart of the issue. Any defense of the unsayable as a coherent and philosophically interesting notion will have to take a stand on the very idea of what constitutes a language. What is at stake in the contentions over the unsayable is our very conception of language. The argument for infinite semantic expansion turns on the idea of THE LANGUAGE, the union of all languages. But is THE LANGUAGE a language? There are reasons for thinking it is not. Consider the union of Mandarin, Navajo, and English. Call this THE MNE LANGUAGE. Is this one language or three? It seems to me it is three not one. Mandarin, Navajo, and English each has not only distinct semantic content, but each also has its own distinct syntax. Though THE MNE LANGUAGE contains all the semantic content of the three languages and so has more semantic power than any one of the three separately, in the simple union of the three there is no overarching syntax or grammar that connects the three languages structurally. Anyone who becomes proficient in THE MNE LANGUAGE will simply be trilingual. Of course, anyone who knows the three languages may be able to express things that are unsayable to someone limited to only one of the languages. So, there is possible semantic expansion in being trilingual. However, what is not included in THE MNE LANGUAGE is any *syntactic* expansion. The trilingual person will have all the syntactic resources of the three languages available to express things perhaps not expressible in one of the languages separately. But THE MNE LANGUAGE lacks a syntax that unites these three, possibly incompatible, grammars. If that is the case, then any translation between the languages will leave something out, namely what is distinct about the respective structures.

Preserving the syntactic structure of distinct natural languages may not be necessary for semantic expansion however. In a Tarski-like hierarchy of formal metalanguages any language contains the syntax of the language below it. It is possible, however, that an expansion of natural languages could involve a kind of syntactic *compression* to achieve semantic expansion. Imagine a language that semantically contains Mandarin, Navajo, and English, but abstracts over their syntactic differences, containing them all in a much more structurally simple, Chomsky-style universal grammar. The result would not preserve the syntactic difference of the three languages but would contain all of them semantically. There would be semantic expansion and syntactic compression. Whether such an expansion of THE MNE LANGUAGE is a realistic possibility is a question of linguistic theory that depends on technical details that cannot be answered in advance. For example, if the formal Tarski-style truth definition for a language does not provide an adequate semantics for natural languages, then any similarity between the formal expansion of language that creates the infinite hierarchy may not be helpful in determining the issue of the semantic expansion of natural languages. Fortunately, as I will argue shortly, when it comes to a defense of the philosophically interesting unsayable, these technical contentions can be left up in the air.

Still, there may be important lessons to be learned even from successful semantic expansion of formal languages. Consider a formal semantics for the language of first-order modal logic in which the meanings of the first-order quantifiers are given in a second-order metalanguage involving second-order quantifiers. An interesting philosophical question arises about how we understand the meaning of the higher-order quantifiers at that level. As Timothy Williamson puts it: "The main problem is philosophical, not technical. Informally, how are we to understand the higher-order quantifiers? Giving them a formal semantics in a still higher-order metalanguage does not answer that question, for how are we to understand its higher-order quantifiers in the metalanguage?"[28] An obvious response would be to paraphrase "the higher-order quantifiers of the formal object-language in natural language."[29]

This move only returns us to the original problem. Natural language treats the second-level quantifications in first-order terms. The difficulty is illustrated, as Williamson nicely points out, by Frege's paradox—the concept *horse* is not a concept.[30] The phrase 'The concept *horse*' acts like a proper name in the natural language, so our understanding of it is as a name referring to an object, not a concept. So Frege's contradictory sentence. Ascending to a higher-order quantification may solve the problem, but natural language will not lend us a way of understanding the second-level quantifiers without taking us full circle back to the problem. Thus the question of how to understand the quantifiers in the metalanguage.

The interesting upshot of the case of higher-order logic is that our understanding of the metalanguage may depend on our ability to master the practice of using them. We understand the metalanguage at each level from inside, as Williamson so figuratively puts it:

> Despite the incompleteness of higher-order logic, the meanings of the higher-order quantifiers may still somehow supervene metaphysically on our use of them, non-semantically described: but the former cannot be read off the latter from the outside. Rather, one must take the plunge, participate in the practice oneself, and, all being well, thereby understand them from the inside. That is no special feature of the higher-order quantifiers; it is the normal case with understanding.[31]

The literal meaning of this metaphorical flourish may be hard to pin down precisely, but the gist of it is clear enough. The formal expansion of language into an infinite hierarchy of higher-order languages will still leave unexpressed something about the meanings of terms that we can understand. Our understanding lies in our ability to use the terms. The formal theory will always leave this out. This idea is reminiscent of Wittgenstein's later work, but I do not need to defend it in detail. I only want to bring out the possibilities, the lay of the land for expansion of the expressible.

SEMANTIC EXPANSION AND A CONSTRUCTIVE DILEMMA

In the end, there may be limits on the possible *syntactic* expansion of language. If there are, then there may well be that which is unsayable in any possible language. Kant and Wittgenstein both seem to believe in such structural limitations, Wittgenstein at the level of language, Kant at the level of thought. The belief in such limitations helped motivate Wittgenstein's picture theory of meaning. The meaning of a sentence, so says Wittgenstein, is a picture of a possible state of affairs. A picture is a particular arrangement of elements. These elements must stand in the same relation as those things they depict. A painting of a moonrise over the Organ Mountains must arrange elements corresponding to the mountain and the moon in an appropriate relationship. The picture must have a form in common with what it depicts. Otherwise, it would be a picture of something else, a different state of affairs. A sentence may not seem at all like a picture. Sentences do not *look* like pictures. Consider, however, Wittgenstein's analogy of a musical score:

> There is a general rule by means of which the musician can obtain the symphony from the score, and which makes it possible to derive the symphony from the groove on the grammaphone record, and using the first rule, to derive the score again. That is what constitutes the inner similarity between these things which seem to be constructed in entirely different ways. And the rule is the law of projection which projects the symphony into the language of musical notation. It is the rule for translating this language into the language of grammaphone records.[32]

Even though a score consists only of marks on a page, it depicts a certain piece of music, a world of sound. The elements of the score, the written notes, are related in a determinate way. This relation of elements is its form or structure. The score is a picture of the music. The rules for writing musical scores contain all possible musical compositions. Like a score, our sentences also have a form or structure. The syntax of a sentence displays its elements in a determinate relation, just as a picture does. The logic of our sentences displays the form of all possible facts. Our logic is the structure of the world.

Since a meaningful sentence is a picture, a strange conclusion follows. A sentence cannot *say* what it means. Wittgenstein seems to offer the following argument:

1. The meaning (*Sinn*) of a sentence is a picture of a possible state of affairs.
2. A picture must have a form in common with what it depicts—its pictorial form: the possibility that the elements of the picture are related in a determinate way (2.17–2.171).
3. A picture can depict reality (2.19), but it cannot depict that it depicts reality—it shows it.

Consider the picture of my cat on the mat. It depicts a certain state of affairs—that the elements, the cat and the mat, are related in a determinate way. But this picture cannot depict that it depicts that state of affairs—its pictorial form—it simply displays or shows its pictorial form. To depict in the picture that it does this the picture would somehow have to stand outside itself and comment on its own pictorial form (2.173–2.174). This is impossible.

1. Since any meaningful sentence is a picture, a sentence cannot say what it means. It cannot stand outside itself and comment on its meaning. It means something but it doesn't say that it means what it means (4.022).
2. We understand (grasp) the meaning of a sentence when we see how the elements are combined. The sentence shows this combination—it is a picture.
3. So, there are things that can be understood but not said. They can only be shown. "Everything that can be thought at all can be thought clearly. Everything that can be put into words can be put clearly" (4.116). "Propositions *show* the logical form of reality" (4.121). So, "What *can* be shown, *cannot* be said" (4.1212). (Wittgenstein considered this distinction the most important insight in the *Tractatus*.)
4. "There are, indeed, things that cannot be put into words" (6.522). [*Unaussprechliches* = unsayable.]

So, the *Tractatus* ends simply with: "What we cannot speak about we must pass over in silence" (7).

Consider again the musical score. It cannot depict that it depicts sound. It simply shows us, via its form, a picture of the sound. Likewise, a sentence cannot say that it means what it means. It simply shows it. It cannot stand outside itself and comment on its own meaning any more than the score can stand outside itself and describe that it represents the sound. We grasp the meaning of the score when we hear how the elements are combined. We understand the meaning of a sentence when we see how its elements are combined. They are pictures. Wittgenstein concludes that there are things that cannot be said but only shown. Inherent in language is that it can point beyond itself to the unsayable.

Wittgenstein's argument is transcendental—what makes language possible, the logic of language, limits it necessarily in a way language cannot overcome. It is exactly the kind of argument that, if it were successful, would show that there is something inexpressible in principle. But the argument with its conception of language contains a fatal flaw. Though we may grant that a sentence cannot say what it means—that is not what a sentence does—it simply does not follow that another sentence cannot say what a different sentence means. If so, then the meaning is perfectly expressible. This is what inspires the idea of ascending to a metalanguage to talk about the meaning of another language. And so, the argument fails. But it illustrates the kind of argument we need if we are to show conclusively that there is something unsayable.

I do not know whether such a transcendental argument for the unsayable is possible. On the other hand, I do not know how we could rule out the possibility. Someone may come along with an unassailable proof. But I now want to argue that we do not have to wait for the verdict. A philosophically interesting sense of the unsayable, ineffable, or inexpressible may be at hand in either case. My argument takes the form of a constructive dilemma:

1. Either language is not infinitely semantically expandable—there is a limit in principle to what can be said, or language is semantically expandable—infinite semantic expansion is always possible.
2. If language is not infinitely semantically expandable—there is a limit in principle to what can be said—then there is something that is unsayable or inexpressible in principle.
3. If language is semantically expandable—infinite semantic expansion is always possible—then for any language L, there is a time, when something is unsayable or inexpressible at that time.
4. Therefore, either there is something that is unsayable or inexpressible in principle or for any language L, there is a time when there is something that is unsayable or inexpressible at that time.

In either case, I will argue, we will be left with something philosophically interesting which is unsayable or inexpressible. First, let me defend the constructive dilemma. The argument is clearly valid. What of the truth of the premises? The disjunction in the first premise presents two mutually exclusive options, and so is justified as it stands. We have two cases to consider. The first is the easy case. Suppose language is not infinitely semantically expandable—there is a limit in principle to what can be said. If there is a limit to what can be said, then there is that which is on the other side of the limit. This will be the unsayable or inexpressible in principle. Another way to think of it: if there is an in principle limit on what can be expressed, then there is something not even an all-knowing, omnipotent God could express. Some might object that an omnipotent, all-knowing God could do anything, even express the inexpressible. It is hard to conceive what state of affairs is brought about in that case. But some would insist that there is a limit to our imagination that God would not have. Indeed, Descartes thought God could bring about a contradictory state of affairs: "God cannot have been determined to make it true that contradictories cannot be true together, and therefore he could have done the opposite."[33] Perhaps, but such undecidable questions about God may only bring out how unhelpful it is to define the in principle inexpressible as what is inexpressible by God. That conception is only figurative at best. It can only prime the imagination. If there is a limit in principle to what can be expressed such that only God can express the inexpressible by bringing about contradictory states of affairs, then it seems safe to set that case aside in the search for a philosophically interesting sense of the unsayable or inexpressible in principle. Barring the case of God's squaring the circle and expressing the inexpressible, a limit to semantic expansion implies in a strong sense that there is something unsayable or inexpressible in principle.

The second case may seem more contentious, though the case is fairly straightforward. Suppose language is semantically expandable—infinite semantic expansion is always possible. Let's first consider formal languages. A clear, rigorous model for infinite semantic expansion of formal languages is Tarski's hierarchy of metalanguages expanding from an object-language as its base. This example of semantic expansion does not take place in time. Think of the infinite hierarchy as an abstract, Platonic entity if you like. What is clearly the case is that for any language L_i, all higher-level languages $L_{k>i}$ will have greater expressive power than L_i. For any language, L_i, there will be something not expressible in L_i. The order becomes temporal when we consider the case of natural languages. Natural languages evolve. Semantic expansion takes time. The infinite hierarchy represents the expansion in time. The language at each level is the language at a time. (If you are a constructivist about mathematics and think of the infinite hierarchy of formal languages at a mental creation, then the levels can be conceived temporal as well.) So, for any natural language L-at-t_i, any semantic expansion of it L-at-$t_{(k>i)}$ will have greater expressive power than L-at-t_i. For any natural language, L-at-t_i, there will be something not expressible in that language. Therefore, we arrive at the new dilemma: either there is something that is unsayable or inexpressible in principle, or for any natural language, there is a time when there is something that is unsayable or inexpressible in that language.

To some, even those convinced by the argument, the dilemma may seem unimpressive. Only one horn of the dilemma provides a philosophically interesting sense of the unsayable or inexpressible—the inexpressible in principle. The second horn establishes only inexpressibility at a time, exactly a kind of inexpressibility that philosophers are wont to relegate to the trivial, philosophically uninteresting. Of course, some cases of inexpressibility at a time are philosophically trivial. But some cases where something is inexpressible in a language at a time are of great philosophical interest. Consider an example of supposed trivial inexpressibility due to nescience, lack of knowledge. Due to the fact that we are born at a time and our language develops in time, there will be epistemic limits on what is expressible at that time. Recall the simple example of "names for animals or diseases that haven't been discovered yet."[34] This kind of inexpressibility can in principle be remedied as our knowledge increases. But to consign all such cases of inexpressibility to the philosophically uninteresting and trivial overlooks the complexity and significance of the role that the semantic and syntactic limitations of a language at a time have on the growth of scientific knowledge and an important sense of how language can show, or point to, a kind of knowledge that cannot be literally expressed or said at that particular time. First, even before thinking about these complex issues of the growth of human knowledge, a quick reflection on the scope of the phrase 'knowable in principle' will raise a red flag about drawing the line of the trivial unsayable there: knowable by whom? Consider the case of knowledge inexpressible in any human language, but expressible only by God. That knowledge would be expressible in principle, but not 'in practice,' at least by us. If a natural language, without literally being able to say or express it, could somehow show or point to this knowledge expressible only by God, this would be a very interesting case of showing what cannot be said. But it would not be, by hypothesis, a case of language showing something inexpressible in principle. So, there is a philosophically interesting sense of language showing the unsayable that is expressible in principle. Such an extreme case isn't necessary to make the same point. Suppose there are alien species of far greater intelligence than us with knowledge that, due to our intellectual, cognitive, and linguistic limitations, we could never express. Yet our language could show or depict this knowledge. This would be a quite philosophically interesting case of language showing what cannot be literally said. It is not inexpressible in principle, since the aliens can express it. Their theories simply far outrun ours.

The example of the aliens' expressible knowledge being inexpressible in practice for us is merely an extreme case of the growth of scientific knowledge. At any time in human history, our best theories stand to future theories just as natural language stands to the aliens' languages. The semantic limitations of Newtonian physics, in 1700 say, make it in practice impossible for humans living at that time to express our best current theories couched in terms of relativity theory or quantum mechanics. Until Einstein came along and gave us a different way of talking about time, we would have thought that it was inherent in language itself that if an event A occurred before B, then B could not occur before A. It would be impossible for A to occur after B, and B to occur before A. Einstein's theory gave us a conception of reality in which this is not only expressible but also true. What was inexpressible at a time was not inexpressible in principle. Some may balk at this example. It was expressible at that time. They could say it. They just could not imagine how it could be true. The point is well-taken but may miss the point. At the time, they could express the two conjuncts, A occurred before B, B occurred before A. Each of these expressed a thought. They were each meaningful. Yet the conjunction of these, though a well-formed sentence of the language, was an inconceivable state of affairs. The sentence was meaningless. It did not express a conceivable thought. They had no conception of what conditions could ever realize that contradiction. It was unintelligible. So, though they could say the words in a well-formed sentence, they failed to express what we can now. It was inexpressible at the time.

Being in the situation where something is inexpressible at that time, and won't be literally intelligible until a far distant time in the future, does not make that situation of inexpressibility philosophically trivial. If a language at a time can show us or point toward that which is currently inexpressible, that is of prime significance. The fact that this inexpressibility at a time is due to current intellectual, cognitive, and linguistic limitations does not make it an any less philosophically interesting case of showing what cannot be said, of expressing the inexpressible. Indeed, it is owing to the fact that any natural language at a time is bound by such limitations that it is so interesting a sense of the inexpressible. So, the second horn of our dilemma is not a trivial sense of inexpressibility. If, for any natural language, there is a time when there is something that is unsayable or inexpressible in that language, then it is possible, indeed likely, that there are cases of inexpressibility at a time that are neither in principle inexpressible nor philosophically trivial cases.

There are many subtle and difficult questions concerning the details of the growth of scientific knowledge and paradigm shifts that provide accounts that differ in their details to explain this inherent sense of historical inexpressibility at a time and how what was once inexpressible in an earlier language becomes expressible in a richer, later language. One is the contentious issue of incommensurability. Do later theories like Einstein's represent semantic expansion of earlier theories they somehow contain, or do the later theories fail to translate the earlier theories without loss, say Newton's or Aristotle's physics? These are interesting issues. How we answer them will affect whether any particular language at a time is semantically expandable or not. However, the answer will not affect the result of our dilemma. To see why let's return to its conclusion. Either there is something that is unsayable or inexpressible in principle, or for any natural language, there is a time when there is something that is unsayable or inexpressible in that language. Suppose some remain doubtful of the philosophical significance of the second horn and hold it is true only in a trivial sense. If we admit the dilemma is true, we may still ask: is the actual linguistic situation we are in at any given time represented by the first horn or the second? Is there something which is inexpressible in principle? Or is it only that for any language at a particular time, there is something which is inexpressible? My answer is that, unless someone can provide a transcendental argument that there are things in principle inexpressible in any language whatsoever—say one based on the very nature of language or thought—the distinction marks a difference that doesn't matter. Without such an argument, we simply cannot be sure which situation we are ever currently in with regard to our actual language. We are always in a limited epistemic situation such that we must admit that at least the second horn is true—there are things in our known languages that are inconceivable and inexpressible to us that it is possible to express in far distant languages unknown and inaccessible to us. Without some kind of proof—what I am calling a transcendental argument—we are always in an epistemic situation such that our evidence for holding the second horn also gives us a reason at the time for believing there are things inexpressible in principle, the first horn. As natural language evolves the horizon of language—the limit of what can be said—forever advances. Whether there is something inexpressible in an atemporal sense or what is inexpressible is only temporal, as language evolves and what was once inexpressible becomes expressed, each new language will only push the horizon further—not overtake it. So, from our limited epistemic point of view, it doesn't matter which horn actually holds. If there is something inexpressible at a time that can be shown or pointed to using that language at that time, there are some things that in a very interesting philosophical sense can only be shown and not said. My thesis is that at any time, there are great literary works of fiction and poetry that do achieve this kind of showing of the unsayable. If so, their doing so is of philosophical importance.

NOTES

1. W. E. Kennick, "The Ineffable," *Encyclopedia of Philosophy*, 4, ed. Paul Edwards (New York: Macmillan Publishing Co., Inc., 1967), 181.
2. Ibid.
3. Silvia Jonas, *Ineffability and Its Metaphysics*, (Palgrave Macmillan, 2016) 4–9.
4. Ibid., 5.
5. Ibid.
6. Ibid.
7. Ibid.
8. Ibid.
9. The example is Jonas'.
10. Ibid., 6. The italics are Jonas'.
11. Ibid. The italics are Jonas'.
12. Ibid.
13. The appeal to popular opinion runs through Jonas' discussion of these important cases. She says: "Many people will intuitively agree to the claim that there is an ineffable aspect to (some) works of art" (6). Sometimes the class of opinions is everyone, and sometimes it is limited to philosophers: "This has led some philosophers to conclude there is no linguistic category capable of capturing a work of art" (7). These claims give us some idea of people's intuitions, philosophers and otherwise. Intuitions may be useful to develop theories through the give-and-take of reflective equilibrium, but they are very pliable until such theories are in the offing. What we need are

reasoned explanations. If some philosophers conclude *p*, then the only relevant question is whether their conclusion is justified.

14. Ibid., 6–7.
15. Ibid., 7.
16. Ibid.
17. Anselm, *Proslogion*, in *The Existence of God*, ed. John Hick (New York: MacMillan Publishing, Co., 1964), 25. Anselm's reference is to Psalms 14:1 and 53:1.
18. For these versions of the ontological argument see: Leibniz, *New Essays Concerning Human Understanding*, trans. A. G. Langley (New York: MacMillan and Co., 1896), 714–15; Kurt Gödel, "Ontological Proof," in *Kurt Gödel: Collected Works*, Vol. III, ed. Solomon Feferman et al. (Oxford: Oxford University Press, 1995), 403–4; Charles Hartshorne, *The Nature of Perfection* (La Salle: Open Court, Press, 1962); Alvin Plantinga, *The Nature of Necessity* (Oxford: Oxford University Press, 1974), 196–221.
19. Jonas, *Ineffability*, 7.
20. Ibid., 8.
21. Ibid.
22. Ibid.
23. Ludwig Wittgenstein, *Philosophical Investigations*, 3rd edition, trans. G. E. M. Anscombe (New York: Macmillan Co., Inc., 1958), §2.
24. Donald Davidson, "In Defense of Convention T," in *Inquiries into Truth and Interpretation* (Oxford University Press, 1984): 65–75, 72. Mark Walker, "On the Intertranslatability of All Natural Languages" (unpublished manuscript). Walker's paper doesn't explicitly take up the issue of the unsayable. Wittgenstein took up the idea of semantic expansion. When discussing his blocks language, he says, "Let us now take a look at an expansion of language (2) [his blocks language]," *Philosophical Investigations*, 5th edition, §8.
25. Davidson, "In Defense of Convention T," 72.
26. Walker, "On the Intertranslatability of All Natural Languages," 4.
27. Alfred Tarski, "The Concept of Truth in Formalized Languages," in *Logic, Semantics, and Metamathematics*, 2nd edition, trans. J. H. Woodger, ed. John Corcoran (Indianapolis, IN: Hackett Publishing Co., 1983), 152–278. See also Tarski, "The Semantic Conception of Truth and the Foundations of Semantics," *Philosophy and Phenomenological Research*, 4, no. 3 (1944): 341–76.
28. Timothy Williamson, *Modal Logic as Metaphysics* (Oxford University Press, 2013), 239.
29. Ibid.
30. Ibid., 240. See Gottlob Frege, "Concept and Object," in *Collected Papers on Mathematics, Logic, and Philosophy*, trans. Max Black et al., ed. Brian McGuinness (New York: Basil Blackwell, 1984), 182–94.
31. Williamson, *Modal Logic*, 259–60.
32. Wittgenstein, *Tractatus Logico-Philosophicus*, 4.0141.

33. Rene Descartes, "Letter to Mesland 2 May 1644," in *The Philosophical Writings of Descartes*, Vol. 3, trans. John Cottingham et al. (Cambridge: Cambridge University Press, 1991), 235.

34. Jonas, *Ineffability and Its Metaphysics*, 5.

Chapter 4

Showing What Can Be Said

The tension between philosophy and the literary arts that Plato left us makes any happy marriage between philosophy and literature sound bleak. However, there are revisionist views of philosophy that reject some of Plato's basic assumptions and make room for literature as philosophy. Pragmatists in particular reject a number of distinctions that for Plato kept poetry apart from philosophy. Often it is philosophers of a pragmatist bent that lobby for the philosophical importance of the literary arts. One such influential advocate is Philip Kitcher, who argues that some literary works should be considered "philosophical explorations in their own right."[1] He says, "They do philosophy, real philosophy . . . The philosophy lies in the showing."[2] What they show makes them serious philosophy, not what they say. With that I agree and urge myself. I also concur with and find instructive much of what Kitcher says about how literature contributes to philosophy. But it is important to distinguish my ideas from his pragmatist proposal. What fiction shows, on his understanding, is not something unsayable, and the philosophical work it does falls within the traditional conception of philosophy that has come down to us from Plato. Philosophical discourse traditionally conceived can say what he takes some works of literature to show.

PHILOSOPHY, CHANGE OF BELIEF, AND FICTION

To explain how a novelist, playwright, or poet can do serious philosophy, we must understand that pragmatists usually abandon a hard-and-fast distinction between reasons and causes, a distinction near and dear to Plato's heart. One reason Plato spurned the poets was because at best they could merely cause a change of beliefs, not justify it. In contrast Kitcher says, "We do best . . . to examine what occurs when someone ponders a philosophical issue."[3] The standard picture "among most philosophers, especially in the English-speaking world" is that "a change in belief [is] brought about through the presentation of theses and arguments, themselves formulated in more or less clear prose."[4] Philosophers have failed to recognize how literary arts can be philosophical because of their bias that philosophy is a matter of giving arguments and reasons.[5] Their view of philosophy as restricted solely to the domain of reason and argument has got to go. Instead, Kitcher proposes

> a broader view of the activity of philosophizing, one in which what goes on in the mind of the subject can involve a range of different psychological processes—including experiments in imagination and emotional reactions to them—in which the texts and sounds that generate philosophical changes of mind can be far more various than the luminous rows of precise declarative sentences beloved by the popular model.[6]

Literary texts can be serious philosophy because of the "far more various" ways in which they create our philosophical beliefs. Kitcher suggests what some of these various ways are: "People appear to change their minds because they appreciate new possibilities, or because they imagine vividly the consequences of holding a particular view, or because they come to realize that something they were inclined to believe 'just doesn't fit.'"[7] Some literary works are especially good at expanding our horizons in just these ways, and when they do so they qualify as philosophical works.

This suggestion does seem to open conceptual space for a sense in which a literary work can count as doing philosophy. But when we see in detail how it achieves this reconciliation, the pragmatist account of fiction as philosophy won't be too different in kind from the traditional conception of philosophy. It may not provide any sense in which a literary work counts as seriously philosophical not captured by the traditional picture. Kitcher thinks it is best to examine how changes occur in our philosophical beliefs in order to determine what to regard as serious philosophy. For Plato this move commits the *genetic* fallacy, conflating reasons and causes, the origins of our beliefs with the justification for our philosophical beliefs. He would certainly reject the idea that philosophy willingly allows the fallacious into its domain.

None of this is lost on the pragmatist. The traditional picture misconstrues the role of reason in belief formation. Kitcher says: "It would be folly to suppose that it [careful reasoning] could support the entire corpus [of our beliefs]." He explains: "For it is not that we achieved our concepts and categories through some kind of special insight into their worthiness—there was no Cartesian moment at which they were rigorously assessed and found to pass muster." They were socially inculcated in us and modified piecemeal. "The human predicament," he says, "is always to start in the middle."[8] It turns out that the culprit behind the standard picture of philosophy is a foundationalist epistemology that "assumes that the philosopher's task is to enunciate premises and draw conclusions."[9] Abandon that and Kitcher seems to think psychologism is an unavoidable fact, not necessarily a fallacy.[10]

I am dubious of anything in the practice of giving reasons and evaluating arguments that presupposes foundationalism. Plato, the defender of philosophy as dialectic, was in no clear sense a foundationalist. You can believe philosophy is a solely rational activity and be an epistemological coherentist. Think of Hegel, who was hardly a foundationalist. The evolution of the Spirit was a wholly rational affair. The activity of giving reasons does not presuppose foundationalism simply because the practice of giving reasons always takes place piecemeal. We evaluate arguments one at a time. There is no other option. But we can still adopt the standard picture that philosophy is about articulating theses and defending arguments, themselves formulated in more or less clear prose, while affirming Neurath's metaphor that in defending and changing our beliefs, we are rebuilding a ship at sea. Consider Quine who introduced Neurath's metaphor to English-speaking philosophy. He is no foundationalist.

Yet perhaps Plato simply biased reasons over causes, assuming that philosophy is the rational activity of giving reasons, reasons for our most basic beliefs and assumptions that put the world together for us. To the contrary, Plato's separation may have a rational motivation. The pragmatist strategy that conflates reasons with causes seems to create a dilemma: when it comes to change of belief either we can distinguish reasons from non-rational causes, such as emotions, or we cannot.[11] If we cannot distinguish reasons from non-rational causes of belief, then we cannot distinguish rational persuasion from propaganda and other coercive changes of belief. In that case, so much the worse for philosophy, so much the better for the sophists. If we can, then we should always avoid the genetic fallacy and distinguish justification for belief from the non-rational causes, however powerful and important in moving us to reflection they may be. Which side of this divide philosophy stands on seems clear here. We are back to philosophy as dialectic and the rational activity of giving reasons, reasons for our most basic beliefs and assumptions. Fiction may well do philosophy by showing, not telling. But the philosophy it shows can be said.

HOW TO REMAIN IN THE STANDARD CONCEPTION

This fuss over the psychologism and the causes of our beliefs comes to naught when we consider Kitcher's characterization of how a literary text, such as a poem or a novel, makes contributions to serious philosophy. His view of literature as philosophy turns out not to place it outside the standard picture at all. He claims there is a philosophical task that literary texts can perform that is different from giving reasons and evaluating arguments. The standard picture of philosophy fails to consider "whether there might be a philosophical task—arguably a highly important task—of reflectively criticizing the concepts and idioms we have inherited."[12] Novels and poems that can perform this task make serious contributions to philosophy. They cause us to criticize reflectively our concepts and our talk and our beliefs as well. But there is little sense we can make of criticizing our concepts, idioms, and beliefs outside the context of giving reasons and evaluating arguments—that is, outside of the context of justification. A good novel or literary work can cause people "to change their minds because they appreciate new possibilities, or because they imagine vividly the consequences of holding a particular view, or because they come to realize that something they were inclined to believe 'just doesn't fit.'"[13]

Consider each of these in turn: *Appreciate new possibilities.* A great novel or poem or drama can certainly cause us to do this. What does this amount to? We come to appreciate some possibility is relevant to the truth of something we already believe or assume. This falls squarely within the context of justification and the domain of reasons. *Imagine vividly the consequences of holding a particular view.* In order to do this, we must first recognize the content of a particular view and then we have to reflect upon what follows from that view, its consequences. Again, a novel, drama, or poem can have this effect on us, but this is still a rational activity involving thinking about the logical consequences of certain claims. *Realize something I believe just doesn't fit.* This can only mean that we have the rational realization that there is a logical contradiction or inconsistency between what we believe and other claims we are now imagining due to reading the literary text. Perhaps this interpretation over-intellectualizes the process. What the literary text may provoke is a kind of intuition that the situation we are shown does fit our beliefs. But if so, this intuition can be put into words. Otherwise, there will be no way to make sense of what the conflict is. If it is to make me revise my beliefs, it is difficult to understand how the content of my intuition is not inconsistent with my beliefs. If not, the question will always arise of why I revised my beliefs.

One way literature can help us to revise our beliefs is described well by Troy Jollimore: "Arguments and theories that confine themselves purely to abstract speculation, and are thus removed from life in a fundamental sense, are in the final analysis incomplete, and . . . what we need are *embedded* ideas, ideas that participate in, and are put to the test of human engagement in the physical world."[14] I agree that this kind of philosophical engagement in literature is valuable and that it occurs, but it is simply a case of testing our abstract philosophical theories against real-world instances, much like experiments in science provide concrete cases to test the abstract ideas of our scientific theories. The literary work furnishes us with a case study. All this philosophizing falls squarely within the standard view of how we should rationally justify our beliefs. Plato would be happy to agree.

There is another way to understand how fiction can fulfill Kitcher's list of the philosophical things fiction can do. Literary texts can provide us with especially artfully wrought thought experiments and, in that way, make serious contributions to philosophy. Novels, dramas, and poems can obviously inspire such philosophical reflection. However, none of these characteristics places the philosophical importance of literature outside the context of justification and the picture of philosophy as the dialectic activity of evaluating arguments and supporting our beliefs with reasons.

To illustrate his view, Kitcher points to Charles Dickens' novel *Bleak House*, which "engages the imagination in powerful ways, moving readers to change their minds about the justice of social institutions they have taken for granted," and "has prompted many to revise their antecedent ideas about obligations to the poor."[15] In the standard picture of philosophy, "this shift in ethical perspective can only be" the result of "the illicit tugging of receptive heartstrings."[16] He suggests "rather than viewing the antecedent attitudes . . . as a well-grounded perspective from which Dickens' eloquence seduces us," we should instead "recognize the arousal of the imagination as essential to a process, one involving further reflection and discussion with others, that lead to a real *advance* in ethical judgment."[17] *Bleak House* certainly does have this effect, *causing* us to reflect critically, and such reflection can lead us to real philosophical advances. Nothing in the picture of philosophy as the dialectic activity of evaluating arguments and supporting our beliefs with reasons would have it otherwise. There is nothing in the standard view that literature can only seduce us to change our beliefs. *Bleak House* can take us into a world—as detailed and rich as the real world—that we have never experienced where we confront situations that highlight the tensions in our beliefs. So we reflect on our beliefs, and sometimes change them accordingly.

BILLY BUDD AS MORAL PHILOSOPHY

Great literature certainly can, often does, present us with aesthetically powerful, philosophically subtle, well-rendered thought experiments. The point is worth making in detail. I know of no better example of literature as philosophical thought experiment than Herman Melville's *Billy Budd*. This perceptive novella portrays a tragedy of moral conflict, rich with all the psychological complexities of real life, that reveals the tensions in our most deep-seated moral beliefs and presuppositions. The power of the book is that the reader cannot come away without feeling the force of what I am calling the "significant moral residue" inescapable in any principled way of resolving the conflict. The force is the tragic upshot of the book. What Melville created in *Billy Budd* is a work of moral philosophy, as much so as any treatise or textbook, albeit one with the aesthetic virtues of an artistic masterpiece.

This description may seem exaggerated or best not to take literally. Consider H. A. Prichard's comment in a footnote to his essay "Does Moral Philosophy Rest on a Mistake?": "If we turn from books on Moral Philosophy to any vivid account of human life and action such as we find in Shakespeare, nothing strikes us more than the comparative remoteness of discussions of Moral Philosophy from the facts of actual life."[18] Shakespeare aside, my reading of *Billy Budd* will suggest otherwise. When we turn to *Billy Budd*, nothing strikes us more in the vivid account of human life and action than the intricacies of moral philosophy embodied there.

The story is set in 1797 during the heyday of British naval power. Billy Budd, a young sailor of extraordinary character, is taken from his merchant ship, the *Rights-of-Man*, and conscripted to serve aboard the warship, *Bellipotent*. His character is of a rare type, what the narrator calls "the handsome sailor," as beautifully sculpted as a Greek statue with a "moral nature . . . seldom out of keeping with the physical makeup."[19] His character is repeatedly described in terms of virtue that commands respect and admiration from his comrades: "Not that he preached to them or said or did anything in particular; but a certain virtue went out of him."[20] Uneducated and illiterate, Billy is innocent and unsophisticated, incapable of duplicity or deceit: "To deal in double meanings and insinuations of any sort was quite foreign to his nature."[21] His virtues "pristine and unadulterated" were born into him naturally, not "derived from custom or convention."[22] Unfortunately for Billy, he is incapable of comprehending badness or evil in others, much like "Adam presumably might have been before the urbane Serpent wriggled himself into his company."[23] This moral naiveté plays a key role in the tragic events that befall Billy.

Though the other sailors all love Billy, John Claggart, the master-at-arms, takes a serious dislike to him. The motivation for Claggart's animosity is initially unclear. The two men shared no previous history prior to the *Bellipotent*, and Billy has done nothing to inspire contempt in Claggart. What we are told is that Claggart suffers from a "Natural Depravity: a depravity according to nature."[24] This rare defect of character was born in him, not "engendered by vicious training or corrupting books or licentious living."[25] Claggart is cold and calculating. His mind is subject to the "law of reason," but his heart is irrational. He is rational only in an instrumental sense; he uses reason as "an implement for effecting the irrational."[26] The passion, "irreconcilable in reason," that drives him is envy of Billy's beauty. Though Claggart is "perhaps the only man in the ship intellectually capable of adequately appreciating the moral phenomena presented by Billy Budd," his scorn for the young sailor's moral innocence only intensifies his envy, and he sets a trap to frame the naïve sailor for plotting mutiny.[27]

One night a stranger from another part of the ship approaches Billy in his bunk and offers him two gold coins, but before Billy even hears the conditions, he rejects the offer and threatens to throw the stranger overboard. This incident is interrupted by a superior who was awakened. When confronted, Billy can only stutter. Though Billy hasn't taken the bait, what unfolds implies that his association with this character gives Claggart all he needs to report him to the captain, Edward Vere, for conspiracy. Vere is suspicious, but has Billy brought to his quarters to face his accuser. When he hears the charges against him, Billy—whom we have been told has one flaw, he stutters when under pressure—cannot speak. Instead, he throws a punch, striking Claggart in the head, killing him instantly. Captain Vere immediately recognizes that Billy has committed a capital crime on the high seas. The captain has two choices: place Billy in the brig until they rejoin the fleet and refer the case to the admiral and a proper naval court or assemble a "drumhead" court and handle the matter without delay onboard. Given that in recent months several serious mutinies have occurred in the British fleet and the tensions are high, Vere chooses to hold the drumhead court, using three officers from the ship to make deliberations.[28] In the debate of the drumhead court, the tensions in the basic beliefs and assumptions of moral philosophy unfold.

All parties in the deliberations agree on two points from the outset. Billy, whose basic goodness they all recognize, didn't intend to kill Claggart, and Claggart, though they can't determine his specific motive, was ill-intended. The captain compares Claggart to Ananias, who was mysteriously struck dead because, as the apostle Peter tells him, "thou hast not lied unto men, but unto God."[29] The members of the drumhead court first want to focus on the motives of Claggart and Billy, considerations that sway their sympathies toward Billy. Captain Vere, however, though bookish and pensive, is a strict disciplinarian with a monkish devotion to his military duty, who insists that they must restrict their case to the naval code alone and leave morality out of it. Their hesitancy to admit Billy's guilt and sentence him to death is the result, says Captain Vere, of "the clash of military duty with moral scruple—scruple vitalized by compassion."[30] Vere shares their compassion and sympathy for Billy but says he must ignore it. Billy's deed "navally regarded, constituted the most heinous of military crimes."[31] In this clash of duty and compassion, the situation already has the makings of a moral dilemma. That the captain recognizes this tension was evident in his initial reaction to Claggart's death: "Struck dead by an angel of God! Yet the angel must hang!"[32] Vere, "no lover of authority for authority's sake," is reticent to sentence Billy without some hearing: "He was glad it would not be at variance with usage to turn the matter over to a summary court of his own officers."[33] Thus, the drumhead court.

Though the ultimate responsibility rested on the captain, he felt from the beginning the force of the moral conflict he found himself in.

The novella, thus far, might seem at best a case study in ethics in which military duty clashes with some other moral considerations. Yet when Vere defends the appeal to the naval code to determine the case, the debate cuts deeper. When Vere sets aside consideration of Billy's intention and the appeal of compassion, he argues that all that matters are the consequences of the action: "Quite aside from any conceivable provoking motive actuating the master-at-arms, and irrespective of the provocation of the blow, a martial court must needs in the present case confine its attention to the blow's consequence."[34] What he means here is that Billy's action is murder simply because his blow caused Claggart's death. So saying, Vere has endorsed a consequentialist principle that Bernard Williams puts thus: "Consequentialism is basically indifferent to whether a state of affairs consists in what I do, or what is produced by what I do."[35] The captain's case is based on the importance of this indifference. As I understand it, consequentialism is the idea that any action, law, practice, or institution that can be justified at all, is justified in terms of its consequences. As the debate unfolds, Captain Vere seems to let consequences carry all the moral weight.

Vere works out a defense of his decision in an almost dialectic fashion in exchange with the members of the drumhead court—though much like Socrates, his interlocutors are no match for him. He suggests several possible consequentialist reasons, before he lands on the decisive and most compelling one.[36] Though his first justification is put in terms of loyalty to the naval code, it quickly becomes clear that it involves a kind of rule consequentialism. What at first sounds like an unwavering commitment to the Crown becomes a defense of the categorical application of the code by reference to its consequences. The naval code, based on the Mutiny Act, is clear. As Vere succinctly puts it: "In wartime at sea a man-of-war's man strikes his superior in grade, the blow kills. Apart from its effect the blow itself is, according to the Articles of War, a capital crime."[37] Vere clearly has retributivist sentiments—the justification for the punishment is looking backward to the action that was done. If Billy broke the law, then he thus deserves to be punished. It is that simple. Yet this sentiment is not incompatible with the future-looking justification of the law that Vere offers in terms of its consequences in war. As Rawls has made clear, "Utilitarians agree that punishment is to be inflicted only for the violation of the law."[38] The concept of punishment implies as much. In a footnote, Rawls adds:

> They [utilitarians] could agree with Bradley that: 'Punishment is punishment only when it is deserved. We pay the penalty, because we owe it, and for no other reason; and if the punishment is inflicted for any other reason whatever

than because it is merited by wrong, it is a gross immorality, a crying injustice, an abominable crime, and not what it pretends to be.'[39]

The captain refers to the naval law as "the code under which alone we officially proceed," and with an analogy seems to suggest it was crafted for, and justified by, its success in war: "And the Mutiny Act, War's child, takes after the father."[40] Its judgment is severe, uncompromising in its demands. In a war where sailors are conscripted against their will to fight to their death in defense of the Crown, perhaps against the pangs of their conscience, they must be motivated by the threat of punishment imposed unreservedly and without leniency. The Mutiny Act defines in part what it means to be a sailor in the Royal Navy, what that role entails. It is constitutive of that role. That role so defined is justified by its consequences—success in war. A Navy with such a rule as the Mutiny Act is much more likely to succeed in war than one that does not have such a code. So Billy must be punished. His act is a clear violation of this constitutive code.

The idea of a code, rule, or role being justified by its consequences comes with an ethical problem of its own, however. Though a Navy with such a rule or code as the Mutiny Act that is unexceptionally applied will have a much greater success in war than one without it—that is, the consequences of the rule will be much better—there seems to be particular cases in which the strict application of the rule will be unjust. Billy Budd is such a case. The issue becomes immediately apparent in the reaction of the members of the drumhead court. The sailing master asks the Captain for leniency for Billy: "Can we not convict and yet mitigate the penalty?"[41] The Captain's response is quick and clear: "Were that clearly lawful for us under the circumstances, consider the consequences of such clemency."[42] Suddenly, Vere has gone from applying the law to Billy because of the consequentialist considerations that justify the law to punishing Billy based on the consequences this particular act of punishment will have for all concerned. The Captain's judgment, initially based on a kind of rule consequentialism, is now grounded in considerations of the consequences of the particular acts of punishment of, or leniency to, Billy. The likely consequences, Vere believes, are easy to see. The crew, keenly aware of the recent revolts in the British Navy, will view Billy's act as "plain homicide committed in a flagrant act of mutiny."[43] Any leniency toward Billy they will view as a weakness in the command, a sign that the captain is afraid of them. It will only "provoke new troubles," the likely mutiny of the crew. These consequences would of course be disastrous. Billy must die to quell any rebellion likely to ensue if he is granted clemency. Despite the goodness of Billy's character and the innocence of his motive, the likely disastrous consequences of not punishing him make it clear that putting him to death is the best overall outcome, much better for all involved, with the exception of poor Billy. In the end, Captain Vere disregards all consideration of motive, sympathy, or compassion and decides based solely on what he believes to be the most probable consequences the act of punishing Billy will have. Vere, though apparently convinced of the moral rightness of his action, never got over the fact that he put Billy, a good man incapable of ill intention, to death. So, the novella ends in moral tragedy. What we have experienced by the end of the story is a clash between our consequentialist intuitions and our non-consequentialist, deontological ones. They cannot be resolved in this situation, and the result is the moral regret Vere experiences. The tragedy is we do not see how Vere could have avoided it. It is a thought experiment in moral philosophy. The result we feel, the intuition elicited, is that any acceptable moral theory, whether consequentialist or deontological, must not only provide an account of the justification of the action, but must also account for this inevitable moral emotion that is the residue of such cases as Billy Budd. Any defensible moral theory must explain the weight of this regret or explain it away. What we have is a philosophical thought experiment in moral philosophy.

LITERARY THOUGHT EXPERIMENTS—
THE THICK AND THIN OF IT

Literature can thus bring us to the rational revision of those beliefs. Thought experiments in science and philosophy sometimes do exactly the same thing. The philosophical force of *Bleak House*, for all Kitcher says, is to provide us with a highly detailed, aesthetically well-rendered thought experiment. This kind of showing that literary texts do sometimes perform is not one that cannot be said.

Not everyone is convinced that novels and other fictions serve as thought experiments. Gregory Currie rejects novels and literary tales as thought experiments precisely because they, as I like to put it, are so highly detailed and aesthetically well-rendered. Currie contrasts proposed cases of thought experiments in fiction with some classical thought experiments in science— for example, Galileo's scenario of falling bodies, and in philosophy, the Trolley Problem. He points out that great works of fiction "are much more complex and sustained and in consequence harder to interpret. But if there is a relative abundance of these complex thought experiments in this area why do we not find any of the more elementary kind, more closely paralleling the examples from physics?"[44] Add to that worry the fact that the aesthetic power of works of fiction often depend, at least in part, on original and compelling flourishes of style. Currie asks "whether the distinctively literary styles we associate with canonical fiction make it easier or harder for them to be seen as epistemically fruitful TEs [thought experiments]."[45] Harder, argues Currie.

These points are well-taken and important, but I remain unconvinced that great fiction, such as *Billy Budd*, cannot be understood as fruitful thought experiments, perhaps because I approach the issue differently. Instead of contrasting the proposed great works of fiction with the simplest scenarios from physics, I follow Thomas Kuhn's lead and conceive of thought experiments in comparison with actual experiments in science. The similarities are fruitful and complicated. Kuhn warns: "No single thought experiment can, of course, stand for all those which have been historically significant. The category 'thought experiment' is in any case too broad and vague for epitome."[46] I don't believe that Currie would deny this point. But I think it is key to keep in mind here. The multifaceted character of thought experiments comes from the breadth and vagueness of the word 'experiment' itself. It is, in Wittgenstein's sense, a 'family resemblance' term.[47] In the sciences alone, the word 'experiment' is used in so many ways that I think it would be hard to come up with something that was both true and interesting about all the uses. Actual scientific experiments fall on a continuum that ranges between highly controlled laboratory experiments to 'natural' experiments, which are neither controlled nor repeatable. Highly controlled experiments are usually in idealized conditions. Natural experiments, uncontrolled by any artificial laboratory setting, take place in real-world circumstances. The former sort are apt to be better at isolating the condition or conditions under investigation, but then there is the worry about their real-world applicability. Natural experiments have the inverse problem. Some famous experiments fall somewhere in between. Think of Einstein's test of relativity that involved waiting for the total eclipse in order to establish the curvature of space. It is not exactly controlled like a lab experiment and isn't ideal. It simply involves observing carefully what is happening in the natural world at a given time under natural conditions. They are all experiments.

Thought experiments exhibit an analogous family resemblance. Thought experiments can do a number of different things and still be thought experiments. Useful in this context is Daniel Dennett's idea that thought experiments in philosophy are "intuition pumps": "Such thought experiments (unlike Galileo's and Einstein's, for instance) are *not* supposed to clothe strict arguments that prove conclusions from premises. Rather, their point is to entrain a family of imaginative reflections in the reader that yields not a formal conclusion but a dictate of 'intuition.'"[48] Dennett thinks they can be perfectly appropriate for doing philosophy, but he fears their potential for "the deliberate oversimplification of tasks to be performed by the philosopher's imagination."[49] Indeed, this oversimplification is the basis of his criticism of John Searle's Chinese Room.[50] Philosophical thought experiments, thought of as intuition pumps, fall on a continuum—from thick to thin—depending on the number of variables or assumptions in the setup. Philosophers tend to have very "thin" thought experiments whereas fiction writers tend to have much thicker descriptions. Thought experiments, such as the Trolley Problem, stand at one end of the continuum to works of literature, such as *Billy Budd*. The former kind tend to have the virtue of isolating what one hopes is the only relevant variable, but often suffer from being too *thin* a description of our moral reasoning. The details of works of fiction tend to be *thicker*, but suffer from having lots of variables in play. This *thickness*, however, should not disqualify them from being thought experiments understood as a kind of intuition pump. Their purpose is to elicit certain intuitions. This is crucial for understanding *Billy Budd* as a thought experiment and its emotional force as a tragedy. *Billy Budd* evokes the moral emotions involved in, and essential to, the case that put pressure on the considered moral views articulated by the characters. It's a tragedy, and only tragedies can elicit the appropriate tensions between beliefs and emotions. This makes works of literature especially important when the issues have to do with moral psychology.

Some philosophers, such as Currie, may admit as much yet still be unconvinced of the epistemological fruitfulness of these thick cases. They may pump my intuitions or emotions, but due to the inevitable detailed style and content of a great work of fiction we can always wonder: "Are we responding to some aspect of the content of the story, or to some stylistic feature of the vehicle of the content?"[51] Of course, he means some content relevant to the philosophical concern involved. I think understanding *Billy Budd* as a thought experiment avoids this worry. On my reading, what the novel presents us with is a deep tension in our moral assumptions—assumptions that represent our best moral theories—and this tension results in the tragic result. The intuition that the story pumps from our emotional response is that any adequate theoretical resolution of such cases must include an account of that emotion, moral regret. Thin thought experiments like the Trolley Problem threaten to leave out that element of moral psychology that any adequate moral theory should account for. A thick one, like *Billy Budd*, is much better at eliciting our awareness of this crucial, even essential, aspect of moral reality. The novel as a whole, with its thick tapestry of detail, shows us. Still, what this kind of showing that fiction can sometimes perform so well remains perfectly sayable, expressible. The philosophy is in the showing, but the philosophy shown can be said.

MALAPROPS, SEMANTIC EXPANSION, AND *SLEEPING WITH THE DICTIONARY*

Literary texts—fiction and poetry—can introduce linguistic innovations. When they do, they can show us unexpected things about language and may call into question our received ideas about language and the world it represents. They can contribute to philosophy and the revision of our beliefs. The philosophy is done through the showing, but in a very different way from literary thought experiments. A close look at the work of a particular poet will illustrate how.

Since the beginning of modern linguistics, philosophers, linguists, computer scientists, and cognitive psychologists have held a common conception of what a language is. The paradigmatic presupposition is that a language is characterized by a finite set of recursive rules that in principle generate an infinite number of sentences. There are a huge variety of linguistic and philosophical theories that cash out the details in conflicting and controversial ways, but this picture of language furnishes the backdrop against which all theoretical linguistic debate occurs. The paradigm is Chomsky's, who set down the idea clearly from the beginning of his project in *Syntactic Structures*: "I will consider a *language* to be a set (finite or infinite) of sentences, each finite in length and constructed out of a finite set of elements. . . . The grammar of L will thus be a device that generates all of the grammatical sequences of L and none of the ungrammatical ones."[52] The idea arises to account for what Chomsky calls the 'creative aspect' of language: "Thus an essential property of language is that it provides the means for expressing indefinitely many thoughts and for reacting appropriately in an indefinite range of new situations."[53] For this reason a grammar must be able to generate ever new sentences from a finite base of elements: "The term 'generate' is familiar in the sense intended here in logic, particularly Post's theory of combinatorial systems."[54] Developments in modern mathematical logic provided the technical tools to turn this picture into a rigorous theory. Theories flourished and continue to be debated, but the picture is entrenched.

One such theory within this framework originated with Donald Davidson. According to Davidson, the meaning of a sentence is its truth-conditions. A theory of meaning is to be spelled out as a theory of truth along the lines of a Tarski-style recursive definition of truth for a language. Though his theory of language and meaning differs diametrically from Chomsky's transformational, generative grammar in detail, it shares the same basic conception of language as a system of recursive rules. These rules describe what a speaker knows in knowing a language: "Obviously, every speaker of a language has mastered and internalized a generative grammar that expresses his knowledge of his language. This is not to say that he is aware of them or even that he could become aware of them."[55] Similar thoughts about the nature of linguistic knowledge inspired Davidson's own version of a recursive view of the rules of language. As he explains it, a competent speaker must be an interpreter. A speaker encounters a barrage of novel sentences never heard before by the speaker. Davidson says, "This is possible because the interpreter can learn the semantic role of each of a finite number of words or phrases and learn the semantic consequences of a finite number of modes of composition."[56] Since sentences are composed of smaller meaningful parts—words—the meaning of the sentence as a whole is determined by how the terms are combined. A relatively small number of words and an even smaller number of rules of composition is enough to explain how we are able to interpret new sentences. Since the rules can be repeatedly applied, there is a limitless number of sentences they can create. This accounts for the creative aspect of language. The competent speaker has internalized a system of rules that, given a certain input, will produce a certain output. Davidson says, "You might think of this system as a machine which, when fed an arbitrary utterance (and certain parameters provided by the circumstances of the utterance), produces an interpretation. One such model for such a machine is a theory of truth, more or less along the lines of a Tarski truth definition."[57] Davidson is famous for championing the idea that "command of such a theory would suffice for interpretation"—that is, a description of the interpreter's competence but not of the interpreter's propositional knowledge.[58] Speakers have no explicit knowledge of these details, but such a theory must be shared by speakers in order to understand and interpret each other. When a speaker, on uttering a sentence, is understood by a hearer, what is understood is what Davidson calls "first meaning." It is the meaning of the sentence that the speaker and hearer bring to the occasion—what we might naturally think of as the literal meaning of the sentence, "what should be found by consulting a dictionary based on the actual usage (such as *Webster's Third*.)"[59] On the common conception of a language and a language user's linguistic competence, the speaker and the hearer must have an implicit theory that is "systematic, shared, and prepared."[60] The systematic demand is taken care of by the recursive nature of the theory, which is also supposed to explain the ability for hearers to interpret never before heard sentences. It is this theory that is shared in interpretation. The speaker and the hearer are prepared in the sense that the conventional regularities—such as dictionary definitions—have been learned in advance. Some such theory—what Davidson refers to as the speaker's or hearer's "prior theory"—should suffice to explain linguistic interpretation and linguistic competence in the popular paradigm of language.

Yet Davidson's point in "A Nice Derangement of Epitaphs" is to call into question this very paradigm itself along with its account of what a speaker knows in understanding a language, concluding "that there is no such thing as a language, not if a language is anything like what many philosophers and linguists have supposed. There is therefore no such thing to be learned, mastered, or born with. We must give up the idea of a clearly defined shared structure which language-users acquire and then apply to cases."[61] The idea may seem preposterous, and many formidable philosophers have argued so.[62] However, Davidson's claim is not that there is no language nor the denial that languages exist. It is a rejection of the entrenched paradigm of language that has governed and guided our theorizing about language. Wittgenstein writes in the *Philosophical Investigations*: "A *picture* held us captive. And we could not get outside it."[63] Davidson thinks we need a new picture.[64]

Davidson's case is difficult and controversial, but it is interesting, in part, because of the recalcitrant linguistic phenomena he draws our attention to—malapropisms. A malaprop occurs when a speaker substitutes, intentionally or not, an incorrect word with a similar sounding word with a different meaning. The Hall of Fame New York Yankee, Yogi Berra was so famous—or perhaps, infamous—for them that his are called Yogisms: "It's not the heat, it's the humility," "Take it with a grin of salt," "Even Napoleon had his Watergate," and "He hits from both sides of the plate. He's amphibious," for example. Davidson claims that "philosophers have tended to neglect or play down" malaprops, but Davidson thinks this linguistic "phenomenon is ubiquitous."[65] Any adequate account of what we know in knowing a language must account for how we manage so to understand and make sense of these.

The problem is this. When Yogi says, whether accidentally or out of ignorance, "It's not the heat, it's the humility," he means, and we understand him to mean, "It's not the heat, it's the humidity." That is how Yogi intends for us to understand his statement. He is successful in conveying it to us. Yet our prior theory, what we bring to this novel utterance, does not allow for this interpretation. According to the conventional dictionary definitions we bring to the novel utterance, "humidity" means the amount of water in the atmosphere, not the trait of modesty or humbleness. Our new interpretation of the odd sentence defies the conventions and rules of any theory we learned in advance. This Yogism presents us with a sentence our linguistic theory is not only unprepared for, but one it should reject. Communication is successful nonetheless. According to Davidson, we develop a "passing theory" for this occasion that will allow us to interpret "humility" as "humidity" for this instance. The mystery is how we are able to do this, since it violates the common paradigm of linguistic competence and what counts as knowing a language. Our passing theory is not systematic, shared, or a matter of conventions learned in advance. It is not as though our passing theory is simply a semantic expansion of the prior language, in this case, English. Our adjustment is a one-off, *ad hoc*, hypothesis suitable only to this occasion. It is silly to imagine this change becoming part of the accepted conventions of English—looking up "humility" in the dictionary, you would not only see the usual definitions delineated, but also something like, "sometimes synonymous with humidity—in contexts in which Yogi Berra is speaking (i.e., Yogi-english)." This example clearly illustrates Davidson's point that semantically expanding to accommodate ever new deviant statements would result in "a new language for every unexpected turn in the conversation."[66] He concludes, "There are no rules for arriving at passing theories, no rules in any strict sense, as opposed to rough maxims and methodological generalities."[67] Our linguistic competence is of a piece with our ordinary ability to adjust our beliefs to fit the ever new flux and flow of our experience. There is no way to reduce this ability to the conception of what it is to know a language on the traditional current paradigm of language. So, Davidson concludes that we should abandon the ordinary, accepted notion of language and "give up the attempt to illuminate how we communicate by appeal to conventions."[68]

What fascinates me about Davidson's discussion here is the insight it affords into the power of some literary works of art and their philosophical significance. Malaprops are sometimes used to artistic purpose in poems, plays, and fiction. Indeed, the term's origin is the 1775 play, "The Rivals," by Richard Sheridan, who creates the character Mrs. Malaprop, who speaks as her name now suggests.[69] The contexts are often comedic. Just as frequently, these are similar to Yogisms in that what is meant is easily understood and can be rendered in semantically and syntactically acceptable English. However, sometimes the use of malaprops, neither semantically nor syntactically well-formed, lead us to a new understanding that cannot be explained in terms of the resources of any linguistic theory of meaning. In some of these works, these semantic and structural mistakes show something philosophically significant without saying it literally. The philosophical work is in the showing not saying.

There is no more powerful example of this technique than in the poems of the American writer Harryette Mullen. Her book *Sleeping with the Dictionary* is a masterpiece that exploits the use of malaprops and other semantic and syntactic errors and irregularities to full artistic affect that extends far beyond the merely comic to the philosophical.[70] All of her poems deserve a careful reading in this light, but the title poem, "Sleeping with the Dictionary," may best reveal her poetic and artistic manifesto. The title describes straightforwardly what the poem is literally about—a poet's practice of reading the dictionary in bed to put herself to sleep, her love of words, and how they inspire her imagination. But the poem, through different poetic techniques and plays on language, is also is a double entendre obviously describing going to bed with a lover. This gives it a humorous tone that is common to many of Mullen's poems. There is a deeper, more interesting and serious subtext.

The poem announces its double meaning in the opening sentence with the malaprop, "I beg to dicker with my silver-tongued companion, whose lips are ready to read my shining gloss."[71] We know she literally means 'bicker' because 'dicker' is not a word in the lexicon. She has made it up. "Dick" is a noun we are all familiar with. Mullen has turned it into a verb. We can't be sure at this point exactly how to characterize the action that verb describes, but sex has clearly entered the poem. Such double meanings occur throughout: "taking the big dictionary to bed, clutching its unabridged bulk, heavy with the weight of meaning between these covers" the speaker is "groping for the alluring word," and "aroused by myriad possibilities, we try out the most perverse positions." This last phrase moves the poem to its conclusion in the last few sentences, where I believe we come to realize that there is something deeper and more interesting that this double entendre reveals. The speaker of the poem is at this point on the verge of sleep and dreams. She keeps a pad beside her bed to record any deviant course her mind may take "from the logic of language." These notes log possible entries in a new dictionary. The final sentence refers to "the poet's night vision," which suggests the key to understand what is going on with her words. They can be decoded like "an acrostic of a lover's name."

Though still explicitly sexual in tone, the end of the poem brings us back to the importance, not only of the dictionary—of words and their meaning—but also to the point of what the poet is doing with them. "Sleeping with," we all know, is a euphemism for the sexual act, a polite substitute for "fucking." What is Mullen's manifesto? This poem, especially in the context of her corpus—when we see what she is doing with words—makes it clear. She is fucking with the dictionary. Through the use of an array of semantically and syntactically deviant constructions—the "myriad possibilities" Mullen creates, "the most perverse positions" grammatically of the words she plays with—her poems display Davidson's conclusion that a language is not systematic, shared, or a matter of conventions learned in advance. Her phrase "exit from the logic of language," reminds us of Wittgenstein, but it also suggests a rejection of the paradigm of what language is, that the nature of language is a set of shared, systematic recursive rules fixed in advance by convention.

The single poem "Sleeping with the Dictionary" by itself may not convince you of this reading. Afterall, it is fairly easy to understand and render into intelligible words. Mullen's malaprops can be understood literally as easily as the Yogisms I discussed earlier. The only sign of syntactic violation is the creating of the idiosyncratic verb "dicker" from the noun. But in the context of many of her other poems, including many in her book, *Sleeping with the Dictionary*, the title poem proclaims her poetic method and mission. In most of the poems in the book, she is fucking with the dictionary and the conventional syntax and semantics of English in a deep way to a powerful purpose. Many of her poems are made of words strung together in ways that are so syntactically aberrant that they, in no conventional sense, qualify as sentences. One of her poems, "Wipe That Smile Off Your Aphasia,"[72] is made up of twenty-two lines that consist wholly of phrases of the form "as φ as ψ." For example, in everyday speech we may say, "as good as it gets." This isn't a complete sentence, but everyone understands the phrase. None of the twenty-two lines of Mullen's poem is a complete sentence. Moreover, none makes any clear sense. For example, "as onion as I can"; "as heartbeat as if"; and "as fax machine as one can imagine." Instead of the commonly expected combination "as good as it gets," Mullen has "as penmanship as it gets." There is no discernible semantic ordering of the lines, though they are ordered one after another. One does jump out, however: "as dictionary as you like," suggesting again the throwing off of the standard semantic conventions. Another poem, "Mantra for a Classless Society, or Mr. Roget's Neighborhood," has no sentences at all, but is merely a list of words.[73] There is not a complete sentence even suggested. The words are semantically connected and intentionally ordered. But there is no definite or determinate way to render what the lines of this poem literally say, what thoughts they express. The words are all adjectives. The first six lines are made up of adjectives that characterize life in the higher classes; for example, line five is: "wealthy affluent prosperous substantial." The last nine lines seem descriptive in some way of the lower classes, often of their attitude or emotions. Lines 10 and 11 comprise the following labels: "troublesome discomfiting disturbing/ destitute impoverished needy." The ordering of these words with their various conventional meanings is in no way neutral. The first half of the title, "Mantra for a Classless Society," is ambiguous. It's not a mantra for those *in* a classless society, but a mantra to inspire, motivate, or bring about a classless society—a prayer for a more just society. It is a poem that depicts social injustice in a way that should make us uncomfortable, but also bring us to some understanding of how those in the lower classes feel. Those in the upper classes are "untroubled complacent" (line 4), "cozy comfortable" (line 1). The lower classes are described in terms of the trouble they cause. They are irritating and painful. The contrast again shows that the selection of terms is not neutral—bothersome and irritating to whom? The answer is clear. The words that describe the lower class are from the point of view of the upper classes, how the privileged think of the attitudes of the poor, especially how they affect those in the higher classes. Without ever saying so, this poem ironically reveals the political power of words and the question of who controls the dictionary. The malaprop that makes up the second half of the title, "or Mr. Roget's Neighborhood," signals the connection between the power to organize words and order society. We hear both "Mr. Roget's Thesaurus" and "Mr. Rogers' neighborhood." *Roget's*

Thesaurus a conventional arrangement of words and, though neither Fred Rogers nor the content of his program was in any way explicitly racist, Mr. Rogers and his neighborhood were milquetoast white. Mullen's poem appropriates the conceit of a conventional collection of words to create a picture that depicts, through its structure, social injustice. Like a picture, there are many things that can be said in literal terms about what it shows, but also like a picture, it does not say or express any of this literally. The insight is in the showing not the saying.

Mullen has a unique ability through the use of malaprops and a plethora of other plays on language to create poems full of semantically and syntactically deviant constructions that resound with the beat of her own original voice. But the linguistic anomalies of her poetic idiolect also expand the language by breaking its conventional bounds and setting the language free. Her prose poem, "Denigration," is a series of seven questions, all explicitly about the inhumanity and injustice of the racism that African Americans have suffered beginning with the slave trade. She uses at least eight words, starting with the title, that suggest by their similarity of sound a refrain of the N-word: "niggling," "nigrescence," "niggardly," "enigma," "renegades," "renege." The resulting freedom is both linguistic and political. Her poems appropriate conventional constructions in not only unconventional, but often conventionally unacceptable ways, that reveal the unpredictability and flexibility of language and make it her own. She is a poet who shows us that language is not at the mercy of the powers that be.

Her poems show us what language is *not* in a way that we can articulate in words—perhaps best along Davidson's lines in "A Nice Derangement of Epitaphs." But they also show us what language is in a way that we cannot articulate in any known linguistic theory. Her work shows us a picture of language that challenges and offers a new picture to replace one that may have held our theoretical, philosophical imaginations captive. Her non-standard linguistic uses reveal and force us to rethink our interpretative presuppositions and conventions. They also reveal the moral and social presumptions hidden in our everyday linguistic practices. These realizations and insights her poetry imparts contribute not only to our understanding of the nature of language but to our moral and political understanding as well. Her poetry—by what it does—shows us what language can do. This kind of showing without saying is in no way philosophically trivial. Not simply does it create examples and provide data for which any good philosophical theory must account. It also gives insight and understanding in a way uniquely done by some works of literary art. Though what it shows can be said literally, the showing does philosophy. Perhaps this much is fairly uncontroversial. That some particular works of poetry and fiction contribute to philosophy by showing the unsayable is much more contentious, if not utter nonsense. To that issue we now turn.

NOTES

1. Philip Kitcher, *Deaths in Venice* (Columbia University Press, 2013), 10.
2. Ibid., 23.
3. Ibid., 14.
4. Ibid. I have quoted Kitcher's phrase "among most philosophers, especially in the English-speaking world" out of order. It actually occurs later down the page from the quote that I have following it. However, it is obvious in the context this is the view Kitcher is describing.
5. Though Kitcher may be right that this view dominates philosophy in the English-speaking world, it should be obvious the idea is as old as Socrates and Plato. If these two were mistaken about the nature of philosophy, then they can hardly be said to be the founders of it, and we should no longer say with Whitehead that the history of *philosophy* is a series of footnotes to Plato.
6. Ibid., 15.
7. Ibid.
8. Ibid., 16. All these quotes are taken from the same paragraph.
9. Ibid.
10. Of course, a pragmatist can recognize cases of the genetic fallacy but insist that we don't separate causes from reasons across the board.
11. I am not suggesting that all emotions are non-rational. My point here doesn't require taking a stand on the nature of emotions. I have argued in more detail for the claim that the conflation of reasons and causes creates a dilemma in my essay "The Irony of Contingency and Solidarity," *Philosophy* 70, no. 272 (1995): 217–41.
12. Kitcher, *Deaths*, 16–17.
13. Ibid., 15.
14. Troy Jollimore, "'In the Voiceless Visagelessness,'" in *Melville Among the Philosophers*, ed. Corey McCall and Tom Nurmi (Lanham: Lexington Books, 2017), 4.
15. Ibid., 17.
16. Ibid.
17. Ibid.
18. H. A. Prichard, "Does Moral Philosophy Rest on a Mistake?" in *Moral Obligation* (Oxford University Press, 1949), 1–17, 12, n1.
19. Herman Melville, *Billy Budd, Sailor*, in *Herman Melville: Billy Budd, Bartleby, and Other Stories*, intro. Peter Coviello (New York: Penguin Books, 2016), 248. (The novella was originally published in 1924, long after Melville's death in 1891.) On 254, Billy is compared to a Greek statue of Hercules: "He showed in the face that humane look of reposeful good nature which the Greek sculptor in some instances gave to his heroic strong man, Hercules."
20. Ibid., 250.
21. Ibid., 253.

22. Ibid., 256.

23. Ibid. Later we are told, "He had none of that intuitive knowledge of the bad which in natures not good or incompletely so foreruns experience" (286).

24. Ibid., 276. The narrator attributes the notion to Plato, but doesn't say where in his work the definition is found.

25. Ibid., 277.

26. Ibid., "Whatever the aims may be . . . the method and the outward proceeding are always perfectly rational." "Claggart's conscience" is described on as "being but a lawyer to his will" (280).

27. Ibid., 279.

28. One of these mutinies is known in British naval history as "The Great Mutiny." Melville spends considerable time (chapters 3–5) in this short novella setting this historical stage.

29. Acts 5:4–5. The Captain immediately exclaimed upon seeing Claggart dead: "It is the divine judgment on Ananias!" (299). Though the allusion is figurative, it certainly suggests that the captain believes that Claggart, in some sense, deserved retribution.

30. Ibid., 307.

31. Ibid., 301.

32. Ibid., 299.

33. Ibid., 305.

34. Ibid., 305. And "Budd's intent or non-intent is nothing to the purpose" (Meville, *Billy Budd*, 309).

35. J. J. C. Smart and Bernard Williams, *Utilitarianism For & Against* (Cambridge University Press, 1971), 93.

36. Before addressing the drumhead court, Vere "stood less as mustering his thoughts than as one inly deliberating how best to put them to well-meaning men not intellectually mature, men with whom it was necessary to demonstrate certain principles that were axioms to himself" (307).

37. Ibid., 309.

38. John Rawls, "Two Concepts of Rules," *Philosophical Review* 64, no. 1 (1955): 3–32, 7.

39. Ibid., 7–8. Rawls' quote is from Bradley's *Ethical Studies* (2nd edition, Oxford, 1927), 26–27. It is another indication of the subtlety of Melville's moral understanding that he has wrapped both the retributivist sentiment and the consequentialist justification into the moral makeup of Captain Vere.

40. Melville, *Billy Budd*, 308–9.

41. Ibid., 309.

42. Ibid.

43. Ibid., 310. "He [Vere] threw out as to the practical consequences to discipline, considering the unconfirmed tone of the fleet at the time, should a man-of-war's man's violent killing at sea of a superior officer be allowed to pass for aught else than a capital crime demanding prompt infliction of the penalty."

44. Gregory Currie, *Imagining and Knowing: The Shape of Fiction* (Oxford: Oxford University Press, 2020), 141. His other paradigm cases of thought experiments in

physics are Einstein's elevator scenario and Maxwell's demon. For a case in philosophy, he also discusses Judith Jarvis Thompson's plugged-in violinist.

45. Ibid., 145.

46. Thomas Kuhn, "A Function for Thought Experiments," in *Scientific Revolutions*, ed. Ian Hacking (Oxford: Oxford University Press, 1981), 6.

47. Ludwig Wittgenstein, *Philosophical Investigations*, 3rd edition, trans. G. E. M. Anscombe (New York: MacMillan Publishing Company, 1958), sec. 66–7, 32nd edition. Wittgenstein explains: "We see a complicated network of similarities overlapping and crisscrossing: sometimes overall similarities, sometimes similarities of detail . . . I can think of no better expression to characterize these similarities than 'family resemblances.'"

48. Daniel Dennett, *Elbow Room* (Cambridge: M.I.T. Press, 1984), 12.

49. Ibid.

50. Daniel Dennett, "The Milk of Human Intentionality," *Behavioral and Brain Sciences* 3, no. 3 (1980): 428–30.

51. Currie, *Imagining*, 143.

52. Noam Chomsky, *Syntactic Structures* (The Hague: Moulton Publishers, 1957), 13.

53. Noam Chomsky, *Aspects of a Theory of Syntax* (Cambridge, MA: M.I.T. Press, 1965), 6.

54. Ibid., 9. See Emil Post, "Introduction to a General Theory of Elementary Propositions," *American Journal of Mathematics* 43, no. 3 (1921): 163–85; and "Finite Combinatory Processes—Formulation 1," *Journal of Symbolic Logic* 1, no. 3 (1936): 103–5.

55. Chomsky, *Aspects of a Theory of Syntax*, 7.

56. Donald Davidson, "A Nice Derangement of Epitaphs," in *Truth, Language, and History* (New York: Oxford University Press, 2005), 89–107, 95.

57. Ibid.

58. Ibid.

59. Ibid., 91.

60. Ibid., 93.

61. Ibid., 107.

62. One such philosopher was Michael Dummett, who took Davidson's claim to task in his "A Nice Derangement of Epitaphs: Some Comments on Davidson and Hacking," in *Truth and Interpretation*, ed. E. Lepore (Oxford University Press, 1986), 459–76. Davidson responded to Dummett in "The Social Aspect of Language," in *Truth, Language, and History* (New York: Oxford University Press, 2005), 109–25.

63. Wittgenstein, *Philosophical Investigations*, 3rd edition, trans. G. E. M. Anscombe (New York: MacMillan Publishing Company), sec. 115, 48th edition.

64. For a similar sentiment see Saul Kripke footnote 56 in his paper, "Is There a Problem about Substitutional Quantification?" in *Truth and Meaning*, ed. G. Evans & J. McDowell (Oxford University Press, 1976), 325–419. "I find myself torn between two conflicting feelings—a 'Chomskyan' feeling that deep regularities in natural language must be discoverable by an appropriate combination of formal, empirical, and intuitive techniques, and a contrary (late) 'Wittgensteinian' feeling that many of

the 'deep structures,' 'logical forms,' 'underlying semantics' and 'ontological commitments,' etc., which philosophers have claimed to discover by such techniques are *Luftgebäude* [Anscombe translates this as 'houses of cards.']" 413. Kripke's Wittgensteinian 'feeling' was spelled out in detail in his *Wittgenstein on Rules and Private Language* (Cambridge, MA: Harvard University Press, 1982).

65. Davidson, "A Nice Derangement of Epitaphs," 89.

66. Ibid., 106.

67. Ibid., 107.

68. Ibid.

69. Richard Sheridan, *The Rivals*. Shakespeare also made explicit use of malaprops earlier in his *Much Ado about Nothing* (1598).

70. Harryette Mullen, *Sleeping with the Dictionary* (Berkeley: University of California Press, 2002). For this book, she was a finalist for the National Book Award.

71. Ibid., 67. The entire poem occurs on this page. It is a prose poem with no line breaks, and so with no line numbers to refer to.

72. Ibid., 80.

73. Ibid., 49. The entire poem occurs on this page. This poem contains no punctuation except the comma in the title.

Chapter 5

Showing What Cannot Be Said

ELIOT AFTER BRADLEY: THE INEFFABILITY OF *THE WASTE LAND*

My thought is this. Certain great literary works, often because of their form or structure, show that which cannot be said, either in principle or at least at a time. If the latter, what they point to may thus result in a kind of irreducible semantic expansion. Let me illustrate with an example. T. S. Eliot's masterpiece, *The Waste Land*, is a poem constructed from fragments that are extracted out of, or allude to, many literary works in the Western canon as well as the *Upanishads*, Buddha, and tarot cards.[1] Eliot's poem successfully points to an emotion or feeling that is not articulable in other, more literal terms.

To see how Eliot's poem shows us something unsayable, I believe it will be useful to look at the poem through the lens of F. H. Bradley's philosophy. I do not think it is an accident that T. S. Eliot jumped from philosophy to poetry using Bradley as his springboard. There is probably no other philosopher whose ideas Eliot—having written his Harvard PhD dissertation on Bradley's *Appearance and Reality*—was so familiar.[2] In Victorian England, F. H. Bradley argued that the ultimate truth about reality was ineffable.

Bradley, though he did not think of himself as a follower of Hegel, developed his own original variant of Hegel's absolute idealism. Though there are many rich, subtle, and conflicting interpretations of Hegel's philosophy and the details of his view are among the most difficult to decipher, his famous assertion—"What is real is rational, and what is rational is real"—supplies a helpful impressionistic snapshot.[3] Reality, being rational, is comprehensible. But thought, by its nature, is dialectical. Any particular thought, say the thesis A, that attempts to comprehend reality is, at best, only partially true of reality, and so implies that not-A, its antithesis, is also partially true. Since reality is rational, and this thought—A and not-A—is not rationally stable, reason resolves the contraction with an improved claim B that contains the truth of both previous claims, the synthesis of A and not-A. Of course, the same fate awaits the claim that B, and the contradiction to which it gives rise must be resolved in another, higher, synthesis. Thought thus advances higher and higher, becoming more and more refined until, rational thought converges on reality, and the two are one. At no point in the dialectic does reason, however refined, capture reality. It is only the dialectical process as a whole that is real and perfectly rational. Rational consciousness, perfected in the process, becomes indistinguishable from reality as a whole. All this, Hegel thinks, plays out in history as the march of the Absolute Spirit or Consciousness in time.

Bradley adopted much of this picture, but without Hegel's optimism concerning the harmony of thought and reality. For Bradley, reality is rational, but thought is not. It will not converge with reality. Reality is forever inscrutable and thus ineffable. A simple version of Bradley's reasoning is as follows:

1. Ultimate reality is non-contradictory.
2. Thought is inherently contradictory.
3. Therefore, reality is inscrutable.

Bradley was as thorough-going a rationalist as Hegel. Reality is rational in the sense that it cannot be contradictory. Bradley states his absolute criterion of reality:

> Is there an absolute criterion? This question, to my mind, is answered by a second question: How otherwise should we be able to say anything at all about appearance? For throughout the last Book . . . [w]e were judging phenomena and condemning them, and throughout we proceeded as if the self-contradictory could not be real. But this was surely to have and apply an absolute criterion. For consider: you can scarcely propose to be quite passive when presented with statements about reality. For, if you think at all so as to discriminate between truth and falsehood, you find that you cannot accept open self-contradiction. Hence to think is to judge, and to judge is to criticize, and to criticize is to use a criterion of reality. . . . Ultimate reality is such that it does not contradict itself. That is the absolute criterion.[4]

This passage clearly commits Bradley to premise 1 of the above argument. Commitment to the principle of non-contradiction, however, is notoriously hard to defend in terms any more basic than itself. J. N. Findlay, explaining Bradley, may provide the best account of the motivation behind this thought: "It seems especially absurd to hold that contradiction not only exists in thought and language but also in 'the world,' since it is the mark of a self-contradictory utterance that it describes nothing whatsoever."[5] Wittgenstein articulated the same idea in terms of tautology and contradiction: "Tautologies and contradictions show that they say nothing."[6] Their respective logical form ensures they are both void of content. If you say, "Either Nixon was elected president of the United States in 1968 or he was not elected in 1968," your statement tells us nothing about history, the election, or anything for that matter. The statement is guaranteed true, but empty. Likewise, "Nixon was elected in 1968, and he was not elected 1968" describes no possible situation in reality. Its form makes it forever false, shuts off all options for realization. And so in Wittgenstein's impressionistic prose, "A tautology leaves open to reality the whole—the infinite whole—of logical space: a contradiction fills the whole of logical space leaving no point of it for reality. Thus neither of them can determine reality in any way."[7] Despite their vast differences in the conception of logic, Bradley certainly comes to the same conclusion as Wittgenstein: reality cannot abide contradiction.

Turn now to premise 2, that thought is inherently contradictory.[8] Bradley's explanation and justification for this claim is complicated and difficult. I am only going to sketch essentials of the Bradleyan setting that are necessary to shed light on one way to understand Eliot's poem. For Bradley, any understanding of reality must begin with what he refers to as "immediate experience," reality prior to thought or judgment. So Bradley: "Immediate experience [is] that which is comprised wholly within a single state of undivided awareness or feeling. As against anything 'unconscious,' in the sense of falling outside, this is immediate as being my actual conscious experience."[9] Though immediate experience is undifferentiated, we feel in immediate experience "an indefinite amount of difference."[10] This feeling results in an unrest in our consciousness that we strive to resolve: "Such a whole admits in itself a conflict and struggle of elements, not of course experienced as struggle but as discomfort, unrest, and uneasiness."[11] Thought attempts to resolve this unrest by making judgments that categorize these felt differences. Its goal is to understand the reality of immediate experience, but any such attempt is bound to fail according to Bradley. Like Kant, Bradley holds that to think is to judge, but to judge involves abstracting from immediate experience and grouping it under a concept. However, judgment is relational, and all relations imply a contradiction. The result of thought is only, in Bradley's terms, appearance, not reality: "The arrangement of given facts into relations and qualities may be necessary in practice, but it is theoretically unintelligible. The reality, so characterized, is not true reality, but is appearance."[12] So, thought, being contradictory ultimately, can never comprehend reality: "Our intellect, then, has been condemned to confusion and bankruptcy, and reality has been left outside uncomprehended."[13] Reality itself is inscrutable, and so ineffable. Where Hegel is confident that reason and thought ultimately merge with reality, Bradley instead is either a skeptic or a mystic, perhaps both.

Eliot abandoned academic philosophy for poetry after his dissertation on *Appearance and Reality*. It is difficult to believe that Bradley's ideas did not influence Eliot the poet. Exactly how so may be just as hard to determine in any conclusive way. It is more than an understatement to say much has been written about *The Waste Land*. I suspect many compelling interpretations need make no significant mention of Bradley's philosophy, though some, of course, have. I will not contend with them. My interest here is in the unsayable and in the literary arts' ability to show that which cannot be said literally and how in doing so it can contribute to our knowledge in a way that eludes philosophy confined to the use of reason and argument and the critical reflection and refinement of our beliefs. With that in mind, I want to place *The Waste Land* in the context of Bradley's philosophy. Eliot, the poet of *The Waste Land*, stands to Bradley's philosophy in much the same way as Bradley stands to Hegel's. Each reflects a distorted, degeneration of the view of reality that inspired it. Whereas Hegel's romantic optimism about reason and reality degenerated into Bradley's skepticism, in Eliot's poetry Bradley's Victorian vision of reality became the ruins and futility of *The Waste Land*. In the modern, postwar world, all that remained were our incomplete, inconsistent, and elusive fragments of thoughts and fractured reality.

In his essay on Dante, Eliot addressed the question of whether and how poetry could not only be philosophical but do philosophy. For Eliot, Dante effected perfectly this fusion of philosophy and poetry with his *Divine Comedy*. If we were to segregate poetry from philosophy, as Plato demanded, then Eliot insists that we would fail to understand and appreciate the greatness of Dante's poetry. The integration of the two is essential to it.[14] How Eliot characterizes what Dante did provides a crucial insight for understanding how Eliot's *The Waste Land* does philosophy though poetry. Dante developed his philosophy not as a theory in the modern sense of a set of principles derived from observation and reflection, but as something perceived. The poet presents us with a vision, not a discursive commentary. Poetry is not a study of philosophy, but we *see* the philosophy in the poetry. The goal of this kind of poet is to exhibit or display a vision of the world or some aspect of it.[15] Eliot in *The Waste Land* offers his own vision, a philosophy we *see* because the poet *shows* us.

How does *The Waste Land* accomplish this? What is Eliot's vision? By the time Eliot was finishing his dissertation, he had become critical of Bradley's philosophy. Having committed himself to mastering it and embracing it, he rejected it. In a letter to his former teacher at Harvard, J. H. Woods from that time, when he was still trying to finish his dissertation, he wrote of his change of attitude toward Bradley's philosophy and how he conceived of his project. He had struggled with the first draft and failed to come to any positive conclusion. So, in the revision, he decided to evaluate Bradley's view and provide a critique of it. Eliot felt the best critics of a view were those who had abandoned that view they once held.[16] Though Eliot had yet to abandon academic philosophy for poetry, I cannot help but think that his turn to poetry was, in part, because he felt it a form of expression better suited to present his philosophical vision—a philosophy that we see, a presentation of a sensibility, not a theory. Two years after the publication of *The Waste Land*, in an article in *Vanity Fair*, Eliot discusses Bradley. Instead of attempting to explain Bradley's philosophy, Eliot says that he intends to suggest its effect upon the sensibility.[17] Exactly why Eliot thinks Bradley's view has this effect is not clear. Eliot finds the philosophy, in particular the theory of judgment, plausible. It succeeds in meeting the demands of providing a rational account of the world, but insofar as it is successful, it shows how little good this success is. Rational thought perfected shows that there is no rational way to comprehend reality. This conclusion, this philosophical success, affects the person who has embraced it. The exact emotional impact Eliot describes as either resignation or despair. In which state the philosophy leaves you will depend on your temperament.[18] Though *The Waste Land* is never mentioned in this *Vanity Fair* piece, resignation and despair are two emotions we cannot help but recognize in the poem. The despair of the futility of existence and any attempt to comprehend it resonate throughout, with the mystical resignation suggested at the end, albeit in Sanskrit, by the mantra of the thunder: Charity. Compassion. Self-Control./Peace Peace Peace.[19] Depending on your psychological makeup, the poem will suggest either despair or resignation, perhaps both. On many interpretations, the poem 'argues for the conclusion' of one or the other reaction—despair or resignation.

The Waste Land presents an emotion to us, however not one so simple as either despair or resignation, or even both. Instead, it exhibits a complex, unnamed emotion not captured in terms of our known psychological discourse and that perhaps defies so capturing or expressing in such simple, abstract terms at all. Eliot did not create or invent this complex state of consciousness, but it may have taken someone of his artistic sensibility and genius to recognize it and display it to us. Perhaps certain psychological states only emerge at a particular time in the development of consciousness and great artists are especially suited to discover and display them to us. Whereas the residue of Bradley's idealism may be resignation or despair, in Eliot's *Waste Land* what is revealed is a complex emotion familiar to, and acknowledged by, those of the postwar, modern sensibility. The sensibility and the emotional state emerge at the same time. Great artists often are the first and the best suited to make it known, show it to us.

To understand how Eliot accomplishes this effect with his poem, we must return to his account of Dante. For Eliot, the explanation was in terms of three structural elements—*framework*, *scaffolding*, and *form*. Eliot never precisely defines these terms and his use of them stays abstract for the most part, but we can glean a reasonable reading from his comments on Dante's *Divine Comedy*. The framework is the allegory—the poet's descent into Hell, his rejection of sin and redemption, and finally, his ascent to God. The relations of the elements of this allegory create the scaffolding. This scaffolding in Dante's case provides a structure to represent the range of human emotions, from the most base and sensuous to the utmost noble and spiritual. The significance of each of these emotions depends on its relation to the whole, its place in this scaffolding. What way the poem is rendered into words is its form, Dante's cantos, their structure and arrangement.

The framework of *The Waste Land* was not allegorical, unlike Dante's. Eliot's vision was not Dante's. They lived in different worlds. Eliot presented a vision for his time. The ruins of Bradley's work provided the appropriate framework to render Eliot's philosophical vision into poetry. What do the ruins of Bradley's philosophy leave Eliot to work with? The Bradleyan framework created by his account of judgment is the fragmentation of thought. The structure of Eliot's vision was this fragmentation, the form of *The Waste Land*, fragments. Peter Ackroyd, in his biography of Eliot, says that Eliot wanted "to make that large statement toward which all of his previous poems had been leading."[20] Reading James Joyce's *Ulysses* (published the same year as *The Waste Land*), which struck Eliot "as 'the most important expression' of the present age . . . prompted his ambition to create in poetry something similar."[21] To achieve this grand ambition, it would have to be an expression toward which not only all of *his* previous poems were leading, but where *all* previous poetry was leading. But where was it leading? Just as Hegel's conception of history as the march of consciousness higher and always higher, each age incorporating and improving on the previous, seemed absurd after the vast destruction of the First World War, so the idea of poetry always expanding on and transcending the past masters to create better, more perfect poetry, seemed a delusion. How could one create something new in poetry? Eliot's thought is that it is not by imitating and outdoing the greats, but incorporating them into your work by stealing from them and using them for your own new purpose and, by doing so, create your own original poetic vision. Thus Eliot's famous aphorism contrasting immature from mature poets—the first only imitate, the latter steal.[22] The best poets incorporate and appropriate the great masters to their own original uses. Eliot invented and perfected our now familiar modern technique of sampling.[23]

The use of fragments in the construction of *The Waste Land* is multifaceted. It contains allusions to and fragments—either lines lifted directly or

Eliot's variations on them—from poems, dramas, or novels of at least twenty canonical writers from the ancients to the moderns. These are the giants on whose shoulders Eliot took his poetic stand. The most recognizable include Ovid, Sappho, Virgil, Dante, Milton, Spenser, Shakespeare, Goldsmith, Hesse, Baudelaire, Wagner, and Verlaine. Several of these—Shakespeare, Dante, and Ovid—are sampled repeatedly. There are also samples from the Biblical books of Ezekiel, Ecclesiastes, and Isaiah as well as Buddha's *Fire Sermon*, which also provides the title for the important last section, and *The Upanishads*. Bits from non-fiction that were important to Eliot include excerpts from Augustine's *Confessions*, James Frazer's *The Golden Bough*, and Jesse Weston's *From Ritual to Romance*. Fragments of myths recur throughout, Sybil hanging in a jar, the rape of Philomel, Tiresias whom the gods turned from man to woman so to determine which enjoyed the pleasure of sex more—whom Eliot considered the most important figure in the poem—and the legend of the Holy Grail, the subject of Weston's book. There are also cuts from snippets of history, Antony and Cleopatra, Elizabeth I and the Earl of Leicester, and of course, the recent war, but mixed with a reference to the Roman naval battle at Mylae. There are also dramatic fragments of dialogue, some lifted from or alluding to classic passages, such as some from Shakespeare, and some contemporary pieces of Eliot's own creation. This list of fragments is only an abbreviation. A huge amount of research has gone into exhaustively cataloguing and explaining the allusions at work in the poem. I note these here only to show how much rich content, fragmentary though it is, they provide in a poem of only 434 lines. This use alone is a testament to Eliot's creativity. But, my more important point is that this is only one facet of the role of fragments in the poem—they provide *content*. But fragmentation performs other functions.

There is also the fragmentation of meaning, an analog of Bradley's fragmentation of thought. Anyone who has ever read *The Waste Land* has to wonder what it means, whether it means anything, or is intelligible. To say that it presents many interpretive puzzles is downplaying the magnitude of the difficulty. Sentences and scenes are often unfinished. There is no single narrative voice. Various voices come and go in the poem, some speakers men, others women, but it is indeterminate how many, whether the transition from one line to another is a continuation of a single voice or the beginning of a new one. Scenes are sometimes so lifted out of context and truncated that it is hard to discern what is going on. Any scene that begins is left unfinished. Eliot uses fragments or full quotations in Greek, Latin, Italian, French, German, and Sanskrit, as well as meaningless birdsongs in the form of onomatopoeia—and the mysterious significance of the Tarot cards, themselves an interpretive puzzle in any context.[24] All these are another indication of Eliot's erudition and sophistication. They have also gotten the poem criticized for elitism and arrogance. However just this criticism is, I think it threatens to miss one significant element the use of all these languages add to the poem. None of them is perfect, has given us perfect forms of expression, poetic or otherwise. None can say exactly what the poet wants to say. The poem must contain them all, but even then language falls short, so the interpretive indeterminacy of the poem suggests. It is again an artistic rendering of Bradley's thesis that thought falls short of capturing reality. We are feeling the frustration expressed by one of the voices in Eliot's earlier poem, "The Love Song of J. Alfred Prufrock," in which the speaker complains of not being able to say what he means.[25] A voice in *The Waste Land* echoes the same frustration. In a dialogue of scattered fragments, a woman protests that her lover never speaks, that she never knows what he thinks. She seems to ask him, since he seems to be unable to express himself, if he does think at all, if he knows anything.[26] Again and again in the poem, language fails. Language, like thought, falls short of knowledge.

The variety of voices and the lack of a single narrative point of view suggests another philosophical point Eliot's poem displays—the fragmentation of the self. In perhaps his most famous and influential essay, "Tradition and the Individual Talent," Eliot explains one of the philosophical tenets of his poetics. His aim is to attack the metaphysical doctrine of the unity of the soul. A poet is not a unified self or person. There is no such self. The poet is only a medium for particular impressions and experiences who processes them in unforeseen ways.[27] The idea reminds us of Hume's theory that the self is nothing but a bundle of ever-changing impressions or, perhaps even more relevant to *The Waste Land*, Buddha's similar critique of the unity of the self. The lack of narrative unity of a single voice with a single point of view displays this philosophical thesis. But it is perhaps more interesting that the creation of *The Waste Land* itself raises the question of unity of the author. The poem is always attributed to Eliot; it is Eliot's *Waste Land*. But it is common knowledge that the poem would neither exist in its present form nor have become the masterpiece it is without Ezra Pound's crucial creative editing of Eliot's material. The poem could have easily been attributed to Eliot and Pound. Eliot dedicated the poem to Pound with a line from Dante that declares Pound the better craftsman. The poem not only displays through its form and content the disunity of the self—that there is no substantial self—but it also embodies it at the meta-level of its creation.

In these ways, I suggest, *The Waste Land* provides a paradigm case of poetry as philosophy. Of course, all of this interpretation is perfectly expressible, sayable. I said it. There are multiple diverse interpretations of Eliot's poem that range from, as Ackroyd puts it, "personal autobiography, an account of a collapsing society, an allegory of the Grail and spiritual rebirth, a Buddhist meditation."[28] All of these are also perfectly sayable, expressible. So, in what way does *The Waste Land* show what cannot be said or expressed? The key is a function of the form I have yet to discuss. I think the poem shows, gives us direct knowledge, by acquaintance of a particular emotion.

Eliot famously coined the term *objective correlative* for explaining how a work of art is capable of expressing emotion. The way that a given set of objects, situations, and events are used in a particular work correlate with a particular emotion in such a way that they, when so used, evoke that emotion.[29] Eliot specifically mentions arrangements of objects, situations, and events that evoke the emotion, but it seems to me that the structure or formal elements of a work sometimes achieve this affect too. We can take a clue from Clive Bell, who tried to define visual art in this way:

> What is the quality common and peculiar to all members of this class [works of visual art]? . . . Only one answer seems possible—significant form. In each, lines and colours combined in a particular way, certain forms and relations of forms, stir our aesthetic emotions. These relations and combinations of lines and colours, these aesthetically moving forms, I call 'Significant Form'; and 'Significant Form' is the one quality common to all works of visual art.[30]

I do not believe this is true of all art, visual or otherwise, but I do think many great works of art succeed due to what Clive calls their *significant form*. This is true of some literary works as well as some works of visual arts. The form of the work is essential for displaying or showing us a particular feeling or emotion which is unsayable. Following Eliot, I call this the *formal correlative*. Like Wittgenstein's example of the musical score picturing the sound, showing it without saying it, the structure of *The Waste Land* shows us a particular emotion or feeling that cannot be said.

The way I want us to understand how the poem accomplishes this showing is to employ the terms of Eliot's discussion of Dante. Eliot insists that any interpretation of the *Divine Comedy* should show how the emotional significance of any particular episode cannot be understood in isolation from the rest of the poem.[31] The *framework* of Dante's poem was allegory. This framework created the *scaffolding* that determined the *form*. The result was that the work displayed the structure of human emotions—the various relations among them and their positions along the overall continuum. As Dante had done for his time with the *Divine Comedy*, Eliot accomplished for his time with *The Waste Land*. Unlike Dante, the framework of his poem was not allegory. I suggest that it was the canon of Western literature, the literary legacy of the past that Eliot had to make his own in the present. The scaffolding was the lens of Bradley's philosophy. All this structure gave to the fragments their form. The result is the philosophical significance I articulated in my interpretation above, but it also performed another function. The structure of the poem shows us, makes us aware of, a complex first-person state of consciousness never before so clearly revealed. In the terms of Nelson Goodman, *The Waste Land* exemplifies that complex emotion.[32] Goodman says that when we think of theories of the world (which he calls *world versions*), we usually focus on those that are "literal, denotational, and verbal," primarily our scientific theories. But this emphasis

> leaves out perceptual and pictorial versions and all figurative and exemplificational means and all non-verbal media. The worlds of fiction, poetry, painting, music, dance, and other arts are built largely upon non-literal devices as metaphor, by such non-denotational means as exemplification and expression, and often by the use of pictures or sounds or gestures or other symbols of non-linguistic systems.[33]

The form of a poem that exemplifies an emotion, at least in some cases such as Eliot's *The Waste Land*, works like the structure of a musical score. In music, this structure is manifested in sound. It is heard. So it is with poetry. Part of the art of poetry is in the arrangement of the sounds of the words. It is, most usually, meant to be heard. One key to understanding how *The Waste Land* shows us something unsayable is to take seriously an essential aspect of that poem—the sound of the words. Eliot, who was later to write great plays in verse, originally conceived of the poem in dramatic terms. It was Pound who "heard the music, and cut away what was for him the extraneous material."[34] Just as almost anyone who has read the poem is frustrated by trying to understand what it means, practically anyone who hears the poem read aloud will be struck by how musical it sounds. Some of Eliot's own lines are as beautiful and powerful as any poetry in English. If you have not heard *The Waste Land* or are unconvinced, the only argument I can offer is to listen to it.[35] The poetic virtuosity and the emotional power of the sheer music of the words is, it seems to me, undeniable. (If you don't think so, I have no better reason I can put into words, which is another interesting indication that there are non-propositional reasons to be convinced of something. It is in the experience of the sounds we are directly acquainted with that support, and move us to, the conclusion.[36]) As Eliot says of Dante's *Divine Comedy*, so it is with his poem. The emotional significance of any part of the poem depends on its place in the whole—its relation to the various aspects of the whole. And those include the composition of sound that the artistic arrangement of the poem creates. So, I think *The Waste Land* exemplifies through its form and content a rich, direct knowledge of an emotion, much as a piece of music can.

This fact alone does not make that emotion, so exemplified, unsayable, or inexpressible. We have names for many emotions as well as discursive theories explaining many of them. Indeed, we have names and an articulable understanding of some of the emotions Eliot's poem manifests. He names two above in his essay on Bradley, despair and resignation. He also talked frequently of boredom and futility. The complex emotional and psychological state exemplified by *The Waste Land* is more subtle than these, taken separately or together. It is not captured in, or reducible to, those terms. And I think that it is not one of the psychological states we have a name for. Art, and especially the fictive literary arts, can sometimes display a complex emotional reality that we simply have no name for either in folk language or science. This deficit of literal designations and descriptions results, in part, because emotions, like colors, exist on a spectrum, where one fades and blends into another. Our complex emotional reality often defies discursive description. Art often captures this and allows us to experience that richness of feeling and complexity. My thought is the same as that "wonderful point about the semiotics of the novel" which the novelist Robert Owen Butler attributes to the great Southern novelist, Walker Percy: "He thinks that a novel for all its length, is just an extremely long name for a complex, evolving emotion that has no name but that." Butler supplies his own personal commentary with an example:

> I've often thought that if someone were to ask me what's the meaning of my novel *Fair Warning*, the only answer is read it again. *Fair Warning* is a 75,000-word name for a complex, evolving emotion or state of being or state of the universe—and, therefore, even what it's a name *of* is not statable. The Maori of New Zealand have a name for a hill that translates as 'The Place Where Tomatia, the Man with Big Knees, Who Slid, Climbed, and Swallowed Mountains, Known as Land-Eater, Played on the Flute to His Loved One.' And that's rather like a novel. To ask, *What does that name mean?* is meaningless. It has no other meaning; the name is irreducible. So too are the novel and the short story, irreducible names.[37]

Though Butler's comments are rich and suggestive, I think what he says about the Maori name is more like a detailed definite description. Unlike Butler, I do not consider the novels, short stories, or poems that I am concerned with to be definite descriptions, however complicated. Definite descriptions are referring expressions. They denote. The issue is not what is meant or what is denoted, but what, as I say following Goodman, is exemplified or exhibited. However, Percy's point is exactly my own. What is the complex emotional state or state of our being that Eliot's poem shows? We can give it a name if we want—*wastelandonic*, but this is just a name for something we cannot articulate. What is it? The only answer is: read the poem. It's that. In this way, some great literary works can show, give us a picture of, what cannot be said.[38] Perhaps, there will someday be a word in the language and a well-confirmed psychological theory for this complex emotional and psychological state. Perhaps this emotion is only unsayable until it is captured by such a theory. Perhaps it is in principle inexpressible and can only be shown by such means as Eliot's poetry. Either way, *The Waste Land* shows us this emotion, brings it to our awareness, by exemplifying something unsayable.

CHARLES BAXTER'S "SNOW": EXHIBITING THE UNSAYABLE

This capacity of a literary work to exhibit the inexpressible is by no means restricted to Eliot's poem. Any close reading of a survey of contemporary fiction will uncover stories that do much the same—show a complex emotion or psychological state that defies description in literal terms, be they colloquial or scientific. Caricature is death to realistic, artistic fiction. Novelists and short story writers are often keenly sensitive to—much more so than philosophers or psychologists—the complexities of the inner lives of their characters and the complications of the circumstances they find themselves in. So, it is no wonder that these unsayable, irreducible features of human experience and the world are reflected in and revealed—shown, not said—through their works and key to their success. A wonderful example is Charles Baxter's story "Snow."[39] It is set in and around Five Oaks Michigan sometime in the 1950s or early 60s on a January afternoon in a "drought winter" in which there has been so little snow that "the spiky brown grass" visible on the lawn "crackled and crunched" underfoot. A bored twelve-year-old, Russell, goes on a date with his older, much cooler, teenage brother, Ben, and his girlfriend, Stephanie.[40] The narrative is told entirely in Russell's voice, focused on—for the most part—his distinctive, pubescent point of view. It is never clear why Ben invites his kid brother to tag along, but Russell sees his role as Ben's "private fool," whose "unworldliness" affords Ben "a chance to lecture" him.[41] The particular lesson that Ben schools him in on this day turns out to be how to impress girls, *snow* them, "that is why he'd brought me along."[42]

Ben's plan for the date is to take Stephanie, along with Russell, out onto frozen Five Oaks Lake to view under the ice a car that had gone through and sunk two nights before. On the drive to the lake, Stephanie flirts innocently with Russell. Her teasing, though, is all in fun, at least for her and Ben. She lets Russell hold her hand, and though he likes it, he doesn't know quite what to make of it or how it makes him feel: "Her hand was not much larger than mine, but holding it gave me an odd sensation, because it was a woman's hand, where my fingers were bony, hers were soft."[43] A moment later, Stephanie asks Russell to feed her a piece of gum, since her hands are otherwise occupied, one in Ben's hand, the other in Russell's. "She kept her eyes open and on me. I reached forward, and just as I got the gum close to her mouth she opened wider, and I slid the gum in over her tongue without even brushing it against her lipstick."[44] The sexual innuendo that is obvious in her action is lost on Russell, and they burst out laughing at him, their private fool. He understands that much: "I knew what had happened hinged on my ignorance, but that I wasn't exactly the butt of their joke and could laugh if I wanted to."[45] At the lake, they walk out onto the ice. Ben, who is "heavy enough to be a tackle on the high school football team," jumps up and down on the ice to prove that it's safe, and the "cracking reverberated through all the bay and beyond into the center of the lake, a deep echo."[46] As they approach the place where the submerged car lies buried under the ice, it begins to snow. Russell is thinking what he will do if the ice begins to break. Ben, it seems to heighten the suspense, has them lay out flat and crawl on the ice until they reach the place where they see the car through the glassy ice. Russell says that he "wanted to laugh out of sheer happiness at the craziness of it."[47] The boys both know that no one died, that the driver got out safely, but when Stephanie asks if anyone died, Ben says, "maybe." Stephanie reacts, edging backward in fear. Ben then confesses that he is fooling with her, and she is immediately angry with him for lying to her. "I just wanted to give you a thrill," Ben says. Ben puts his arm around her, she whispers something in his ear, and he whispers something to her in return. He has a new plan. He is going to drive his car out onto the ice and take Stephanie home across the frozen lake. Russell wonders at the bad judgment of teenagers, and though he says he will walk home, he is obviously tempted by the excitement: "Bad judgment of this kind was starting to interest me; it was becoming a powerful antidote to boredom, which seemed worse."[48] With Ben gone for his car, Stephanie asks Russell if he thinks Ben is interested in her. Russell doesn't quite understand her question, but it makes him uncomfortable. He answers literally, yes, since Ben is interested in a lot of things. Their conversation is interrupted as Ben fishtails his car out onto the lake, cutting donuts on the ice. Russell understands that Ben "was having a thrill and would soon give Stephanie another thrill by driving her home across ice that might break at any time. Thrills did it, whatever it was. Thrills led to other thrills."[49]

At this point in the story, just when we expect something bad to happen, that Ben and Stephanie will go through the ice on their fated drive and Russell's innocence will be crushed by tragedy, Baxter does something more unexpected and less dramatic, and certainly without even a whiff of the melodrama a lesser writer might have appealed to. A much older, thoroughly mature, adult Russell interrupts the story he has been telling. They didn't go through the ice and drown on the way home. They broke up a few weeks later. Russell still occasionally talks to Stephanie who, it turns out, has had a fairly mundane life. She still lives in Five Oaks, works as a clerk at the post office, has been married twice, had a few children, even adopted a Korean baby. Then just as suddenly as we have come to realize the story has been told by the retrospective older Russell reflecting on an episode from his youth, we are back to the events of that day on the lake.

Before Ben picks her up in his car to drive her home, Stephanie continues to talk with Russell. She complains that Ben doesn't notice her and asks Russell how she can get Ben to notice her. In his twelve-year-old innocence, a most literal answer pops out of his mouth—"take off your shoes."[50] If we are not surprised enough by Russell's advice—much more so than if Baxter had them melodramatically go through the ice—we didn't see it coming when she follows his advice and takes off her shoes and socks there on the snowy ice. At the sight of her feet with their painted toenails on the bare ice, Russell is struck by the "desperate and beautiful sight."[51] When he asks her how it feels, she tells him he'll know in a few years. Ben picks up Stephanie, and Russell makes the long walk home as night falls. The story ends with a small, poignant act. Russell, outside his house, removes his glove and sticks his bare hand into the snow, as though he wants to feel what Stephanie felt. He holds his hand there until he can stand it no longer, then the story ends as he goes into the warmth of the house.

It is easy to read this short tale as a simple coming-of-age story with a number of familiar emotions that are easy to spot. Boredom, excitement, fear, anger, and desire all recur and are present or at least hinted at. But to read the story as simply a portrait of a naïve boy on the verge of puberty coming to terms with these emotions as he begins the long merge toward maturity into the foreign adult world would be too simple. It would miss the special power of the story and the understanding it lends. The aesthetic key to this insight turns on the moment near the end when we realize that the story is being told in retrospect. Middle-aged Russell is recalling and reflecting on an afternoon twelve-year-old Russell experienced long ago. Early in the story young Russell wonders if fifty years later he would ever remember anything about this day. By the end of the story, we know the answer to young Russell's question. Indeed, he does remember it, and we know in what terms—in the exact details in which older Russell renders the story. Like the older Russell, we understand what young Russell feels that day, that experience only an adolescent can feel. What is it? When we try to pinpoint it, we find that we can't quite articulate it. It is neither boredom, fear, anger, desire, excitement, nor the simple conjunction of these. It is a complex emotion for which we don't have a name. Try to describe it and it defies our grasp. My summary of the story cannot capture it. The way the story manages to perform this feat—though the exact details and word choice with which Baxter creates the twelve-year-old character and relates the events are crucial—is in part due to its form, the way it is structured. The revelation near the end, that a retrospective narrator, the older Russell reflecting back, is the one telling the story, works the magic.

One way to make this point clear is to consider whether my summary of the story should have come with a spoiler alert. After all, I did give away the surprise on which the story's force hinges. Most of you probably have never read Baxter's story, but I contend that knowing the ending cannot diminish the power of the story for you if you were to read it. This is unlike what would happen if they had gone through the ice and drown at the end. A summary of such a melodrama would need a spoiler alert. Revealing that surprise tragedy would ruin the whole story for any reader. We would know to expect the shocking tragedy. But in this case, knowing the ending won't take away from the artistic effectiveness of the story. Any reader, whether they have been tipped off to expect the retrospective voice at the end or not, will *recognize* the feeling that the story captures and displays. Readers may or may not experience this feeling as a result of reading the story, but I expect most will not. Though they recognize the complex feeling, what it is like to feel what Russell feels, when asked what that feeling is, I suspect, their best answer will be, "Just like *that*," and point to Baxter's story. Notice also that the older Russell who narrates the story is in a similar position to the reader. Like the reader, the mature Russell can only remember what it was like to be that twelve-year-old boy. He sees and understands himself from a third-person sort of distance. The younger Russell is other than, different from the adult Russell.[52] The complex emotional state he relates is one he is acquainted with, but one that defies any more reductive description than the one he relates in telling his story, a story that is, in fact, not a description at all but a display or showing of that emotion. If we ask Russell what it is, all he can do is say, "It is this . . . " and then tell the story exactly as he, or in fact, Baxter, the writer, renders it, so artistically as to put on display, show, or exhibit this complex emotion that cannot be put into more literal terms. His story shows what cannot be said.

Those of a scientistic bent may be convinced that there will someday be a precise description of this emotion in terms of neurophysiology, and perhaps they are right and their confidence will be confirmed. Or perhaps it won't and these complex psychological stages and our understanding of them will always outrun the limits of science and the refinements of language. Either way, it is out ahead of these limits that literature sometimes works, showing us, exhibiting to us through language that which cannot be said.

DANTE, CAVELL, AND *THE SOUND AND THE FURY*: FICTION AS PHILOSOPHY

Whether this showing of the unsayable is ineffable in principle or only for a time does not make it any more or less philosophically significant. It may in fact be crucial to new scientific discovery and the growth of our discursive, theoretical knowledge. The arts, in this case, the literary arts, no less than the sciences can, in Goodman's words, "take and unmake and remake and retake familiar worlds, recasting them in remarkable and sometimes recondite but eventually recognizable—that is *re-cognizable*—ways."[53] Eliot's poem may recognize and so conceptualize what was before unsayable. Or perhaps what it shows is unsayable in principle. Either way, its philosophical significance is, as profound as it is, at least for now, mysterious. So, I conclude, concurring with Goodman, that the arts, in this case especially the literary arts, "must be taken no less seriously than science as modes of discovery, creation, and enlargement of our knowledge in the broad sense of the advancement of understanding and thus that the philosophy of art [I would add literature] should be conceived as an integral part of metaphysics and epistemology."[54] This conclusion was one Plato could not abide. Perhaps he should have. Why exactly?

Those skeptical of this expansion of philosophy to include literary works, such as Eliot's poem and Baxter's short story, may agree that the arts might lead to new discoveries that extend our knowledge and still question whether that alone is enough to make them of a piece with philosophy. Why does the mere creation of knowledge or insight make this knowledge or insight *philosophy*? Physics and chemistry make important and steady contributions to the progress and growth of knowledge, but we nonetheless distinguish them from philosophy proper. The arts, including the literary arts, seem no different in this respect. For Goodman, an answer might be available in his pragmatism and the holism it entails. Much like Quine, who insisted that there was no "first philosophy" in principle distinct and separate from the particular sciences, Goodman simply widens the scope of our knowledge to encompass the arts. So, he concludes that all these epistemological endeavors are pieces of philosophy. They all contribute to the tapestry that is our picture of the world.

Such considerations may be enough to broaden our conception of philosophy to include the literary arts—poetry, fiction, and plays—but I have other altogether different considerations I would like to suggest. One key insight is found if we return to Dante and Eliot's explanation of how Dante, better than any other poet, succeeded in doing philosophy in poetry. Thus far, I have focused only on Eliot's early essay on Dante in *The Sacred Wood*. Though Eliot changed his views on many things as he matured as a poet and critic, and finally into a playwright, his praise for Dante as well as his understanding of his importance, as a philosophical poet, never changed but only became more refined. In his later essay, "What Dante Means to Me," written almost thirty years after the first Dante essay, his argument from *The Sacred Wood* becomes refined and clearer.[55] His reading of Dante is crucial to an understanding of why literature that shows the unsayable contributes to, and is part of, philosophy and the philosophical project.

Eliot always regarded Dante's ability to reveal the full range of human emotions in his poetry as one of his greatest artistic gifts. In the later essay, Eliot makes clear what he thinks was special about Dante that allowed him to accomplish this better than any other poet. First, he had to have the ability to perceive more clearly than ordinary people and experience emotional subtleties that they can hardly feel or recognize without the help of the poet. Second, because normal human beings are only vaguely aware of these subtleties they are feeling, we have no words for these emotional states. The average person can recognize them and grasp them only with the help of the poet. Third, the poet must have a clear perception of the reality that the average consciousness is already *acquainted with*. This ability is necessary in order to expand the ordinary consciousness through the creative use of language to a more refined awareness, recognition, and understanding. Fourth, the only way to do this is to develop language and find words that will reveal or show the inexpressible or unsayable.[56] By creating these innovations in language and adding to our lexicon, the poet shows how much can be done with words.

In *The Divine Comedy*, Dante coined a number of new words and expanded the Italian language. Perhaps the most interesting to my concerns—one Eliot calls our attention to—occurs in Canto I of the *Paradiso*. In this opening canto, Dante tells us he has ascended into heaven and experienced a revelation of the Divine Light, but now that he has descended back into this world, when he tries to relate what he saw, the intellect fails him, and he cannot put it into words. It is only in poetry that he can render it, and he prays for poetic inspiration. He recounts Beatrice guiding him into heaven. His experience, as he looks upward toward her and into the light, he compares to that of Glaucus, who in Ovid's *Metamorphoses* ate an herb that changed him into a sea god. Then, in one of the most extraordinary lines of the poem, Dante says of this experience: "passing beyond humanity may not be set forth in words: therefore let the example suffice any for whom grace reserves that experience."[57] Experience of the divine, in any literal sense, cannot be put into words. The example Dante is referring to is Glaucus' experience of the divine after eating the herb. The reader, however, has no herb, only Dante's poem. The poem as a whole must suffice to display or exhibit the experience. Anyone who thus becomes aware of or grasps this experience has not done so through the intellect but by some inarticulable recognition of the experience shown by the poem. To say in words, albeit poetry, what he was trying *to do* in the poem, Dante coined the verb "trasumanar," to pass beyond humanity, to pass beyond what human language can express. This new Italian word, a compound formed from the noun *umano*, human, and the prefix, *tras*, has come into English as the transliterated *transhuman*. According to Eliot, it is from Dante's example that we can understand what literature is capable of. It provides, using Kant's terms, a *negative* expansion. It is a negative term for what cannot be said, not a positive description. This kind of showing what cannot be said is in no way trivial, but gives us insight and understanding in a way uniquely done by some works of literary art. Literature can sometimes show us, through words, the unsayable, something beyond words. And so it may inspire the growth in the future of knowledge inexpressible, inarticulable, and unimaginable now. For Eliot, this gift made Dante the greatest of poets. Dante was clearly his poetic paradigm and the purest exemplar of this poetic genius. Eliot, too, had similar gifts.

Suppose the knowledge and awareness we sometimes gain from literary works is a kind of knowledge by acquaintance of a complex, inexpressible psychological state. Still, it is incumbent on me to explain why such literary achievements are philosophy or the doing of philosophy. I have so far focused on the idea that some works of literature can show us through the creative use of words something inexpressible, make us aware of it, recognize it. The literary works *exhibit* it. I take the term "exhibit" from Stanley Cavell's discussion of the epistemology of conscious experience, in particular pain. We commonly think of ourselves as *knowing* for *certain* our own first-person experiences because we are directly acquainted with them. But when we try to express this thought, we don't exactly succeed, we don't quite mean what we say. How is that? Cavell claims, "'I know I am in pain' is not an expression of certainty . . . it is an exhibiting of the object about which someone else may be certain."[58] More precisely and to my point, it is "an exhibiting of the *object* of knowledge."[59] Similarly, some literary works, such as Eliot's *The Waste Land*, Dante's *Divine Comedy*, and Baxter's "Snow," *exhibit* a complex psychological state with which we are acquainted, even if faintly and without being able to articulate it. We become aware of it as displayed by the work of art and recognize it. It is *that.*

Furthermore, when we witness someone exhibiting pain, say, either in speech or other behavior, and say "I know you are in pain," Cavell claims we are not expressing *certainty*. It is not as though I can ever be sure that what you are experiencing, your conscious experience, is the same as mine. Instead, we are responding to your exhibiting. We *recognize* that state you are *exhibiting* and sympathize with you when we say, "I *know* you are in pain." Our statement reflects our sympathy. We *acknowledge* you as a person other than we are, a person capable of experiencing what you are exhibiting. Must we feel this pain? Must we sympathize with it? Not necessarily, but if we do not, we fail to *acknowledge* you.[60] Literary works may also use words to exhibit complex experiences beyond literal description. When we recognize the experiences as ones we are acquainted with, however vaguely, we become aware of them as experiences others have and in doing so acknowledge them as separate from us, others with whom we can empathize, sympathize, and otherwise feel for, or not. Some literary works, by exhibiting the inexpressible through the use of words, can bring us to this awareness, this understanding.

The verb "to know" has a number of uses. It connotes, for Cavell, at least, these two distinct and philosophically important senses—knowing and acknowledging. The sense of *knowing* is the familiar notion that ranges from certainty to rational grounds and epistemological justification. Knowing in this sense is propositional. *Acknowledging* others must precede any rational reflection on others, their existence, and the epistemological status of their conscious states. It is based on a non-propositional acquaintance with them and their experiences as only we can know them.[61] Literature, in showing the unsayable, can extend and expand our acknowledgment of others, their pain and suffering as well as their pleasures and contentment and all the uncharacterizable subtleties in between. This kind of understanding is crucial to the success of the project of philosophy traditionally conceived as far back as Plato. Its goal is to attain knowledge—of oneself and the world—that provides an understanding of what constitutes a good life for each individual and the best society for all collected together. The method for reaching these goals has been thought of as the rigorous critique of our beliefs, explicating and defending them with careful reasoning and clear arguments. The resulting knowledge, or at least justified beliefs, would of course be discursive and theoretical—*propositional* knowledge. Suppose, however, that some works of fiction and poetry afford us understanding by acquainting us directly with inexpressible states of consciousness. When we become aware of these states, and recognize them, we acknowledge others and sympathize with them. This knowledge is *non-propositional*. It is necessary to expanding our understanding of others and fully including them in our moral reality. The acknowledgment that accompanies this understanding is presupposed in our rational, theoretical discourse. In making this kind of contribution, literature—in the form of poetry, fiction, and drama—plays a crucial role in completing or fulfilling the philosophical task. As Cavell aptly puts it: "In appealing from philosophy to . . . literature, I am not seeking illustrations for truths philosophy already knows, but illumination of philosophical pertinence that philosophy alone has not surely grasped—as though an essential part of its task must work behind its back. I do not understand such appeals as 'going outside' philosophy."[62] Literature does not simply lend examples to a philosophical purpose; it sometimes does philosophy. In some of its forms, it is crucial to the completion of the philosophical project. The understanding it can lend is critical to the fulfillment of its basic goals.

A look at another literary masterpiece, William Faulkner's *The Sound and the Fury*, will help bring these conclusions home. As with Eliot's *The Waste Land*, Faulkner's work shows what cannot be said through the use of its form. The formal techniques that Faulkner employs in the novel create a formal correlative for the point he is trying to show and that the novel fails literally to say. Faulkner, who was highly influenced by Eliot's aesthetics and poetry, especially *The Waste Land*, is like Eliot, trying to write about the complex emotions of all people. He is not writing about or expressing his own grief or suffering, for example. He leaves his own inner life out of it. His artistic greatness is that he can recognize the inner lives of others and exhibit the complexities of their grief and suffering so powerfully in words. In his biography of Faulkner, Jay Parini explains: "For him, a novelist answered the highest calling, entering a priesthood of sorts, and the work of the writer was to take on the suffering of humanity and transform this suffering into art."[63] Faulkner leaves himself and his feelings out of it. Parini continues, "Like T.S. Eliot, he also believed in the impersonality of art and refused to write autobiographically: . . . one simply can't look at any published work of his and say, 'There's Faulkner.' He remains like God: nowhere to be found, but everywhere in evidence."[64] Much like Eliot says of Dante, Faulkner can recognize, even better than the people themselves, what they are feeling and display it in a way that they, who are only vaguely aware of having these feelings, cannot. Faulkner accomplishes this through the creative and innovative use of form.

The Sound and the Fury is a novel set in Mississippi in the first two decades of the twentieth century. The story reflects the decline of the once aristocratic Compson family and their moral degeneration. The three brothers—Benjy, Quentin, and Jason—have all been since childhood obsessed with their sister Caddy and her emerging sexuality. When Caddy loses her virginity, Benjy and Quentin are both in their own ways distraught. Caddy eventually becomes pregnant, is married after the fact, and subsequently banished from the family. The severely cognitively disabled Benjy loses the only person in the family who has ever cared for him. Quentin leaves the South to attend Harvard but is so depressed on the eve of Caddy's wedding that he kills himself by jumping off a bridge. After their parents have passed away, Jason, who has always been disgusted by Caddy, is the person left to take care of the family, including Caddy's now teenage daughter, Quentin. He takes out his vengeance on Caddy by stealing the money she sends to support her daughter. Quentin, when she realizes what has been going on, snatches the money Jason has been hiding and runs away. Jason pursues her, and though he catches up with her on Easter Sunday, he takes a beating from a circus hand who is with Quentin and she escapes. At the same time, and in contrast to the chase, Dilsey, the family's black servant, with Benjy in tow attends the Easter service at her church, where she undergoes a kind of mystical experience. The book ends with Benjy upset because he is being driven by a young servant the wrong way around the square. Jason intervenes, takes control of the reins, and sets the wagon on the opposite course, and Benjy immediately calms down. That is the main storyline, what storyline there is.

The novel takes on the familiar themes of the Southern Novel—traditional values lost along with land and wealth, class differences and their collapse, racism, incest, commercialism, hypochondria, paranoia, madness, and the mentally deficient. But in no other way is this novel like a typical Southern novel. Much like Eliot's poem, it is a challenge to read, and anyone who reads it will be struggling to figure out what it *means*. The title is an allusion to a passage in Shakespeare's Macbeth, which announces the interpretive problem of the novel poetically: it is a tale "full of sound and fury, signifying nothing."[65] The problem the novel presents is that it does not mean anything that can be put literally into words. Though the sentences it is made of are meaningful, the novel as a whole defies meaning. It is constructed in four parts, each told from a radically different point of view. None of the parts connect to the others, except through associations of the characters and events. Taken together they cannot and don't complete the story. It has no arch. The critic Donald Kartiganer, who takes this interpretive problem to be the point of the novel, summarizes the issue nicely: "None of the four tales speaks to the other, each imagined order cancels the one that precedes it. Truth is the meaningless sum of four items that seem to have no business being added."[66] The success and power of the novel is not in what it *means* but what it *shows*.

The tale is told, in so far as it is 'told' at all, by the three Compson brothers, Benjy, Quentin, and Jason, with an omniscient narrator that focuses on the family's black servant Dilsey in the last section. The first three sections are told from the extremely subjective points of view of the brothers. The first two, those of Benjy and Quentin, are both pure stream of consciousness. The third, though in Jason's perspective and in his voice, is more readable. The final section, Dilsey's section, is in a familiar omniscient point of view and is the most traditional in style. Benjy's section is constructed from his impressions arranged in no linear order so that the result is almost incomprehensible. Benjy does not experience time. There is no past and no future in his experience. All his impressions are equally present and void of interpretation. What order they have is based on his sensuous or emotional associations. Quentin's experience, in contrast, is dominated by his obsession with time, an obsession he is free from only when he kills himself. Quentin cannot bear Caddy's loss of what he sees as her virtue. In order to save it, he wants her to lie and say they committed incest and marry him. As Kartiganer says of Quentin: He "wants nothing more than to replace *life* with interpretation. *Reality* for Quentin is primarily change—in particular the change implicit to the sexual identity of his sister Caddy—and interpretation . . . is the ground of permanence in which change is eliminated."[67] In the Jason section, events are filtered through his lens of paranoia, rationalization, and self-pity. Though his section is more accessible and he appears to be much more normal, "his existence," as Kartiganer characterizes it, "is actually a chaos of confused motion, utter disorder within the mind."[68] The Dilsey section is the only one told from a traditional omniscient third-person point of view. It reads like an ordinary novel. The form of this section, in just the way a traditional novel would, seems to create the possibility of tying the meaning of the novel up neatly, completing the arch, and allowing the reader to realize a meaningful, articulable conclusion to the story. But this section, too, fails to do so. The only place in the novel where there is any moment of epiphany is Dilsey's mystical religious revelation during the Easter service. She is struck by an insight and tears roll down her face. What she experiences is not put into words. For Dilsey, words are not necessary. At that moment she knows directly. But the reader does not. Though in a traditional novel this moment might be the pivotal event that determines the significance of all other events in the story, it fails to do any such thing in the formal context Faulkner has purposely and brilliantly set it. After this brief moment, the events and the lives of the Compsons move on in their usual way to the end. In the end, Jason takes control of the reins and sets the wagon back on the same course around the square as the family has always taken Benjy. Nothing is changed and nothing is redeemed. At least, we are left wondering as much. Even this traditional narrative attempt to complete and express the meaning of the novel fails. As Kartiganer says, "In this fourth attempt to tell the story we are still faced with the problems of the first three, namely a failure of significant form, and therefore, meaning."[69]

The formal techniques of the novel fail to determine any expressible meaning, but the power of the novel and its philosophical significance is in what it shows. As with Eliot's *The Waste Land*, the form shows the complex inner lives of the characters, complex psychological states that cannot be expressed in neat literal terms. They are exhibited to us and we are acquainted with them; we become aware of them as they are displayed only in the context of the novel as a whole. The form of each narrative mirrors the structure of their respective conscious lives, their subjective relations to the world. To describe Benjy's world as an "unmediated vision of pure presence," Quentin's as an "effete escapism that seeks a reality dictated beyond the word," and Jason's as a "subjectivism crippled by paranoia" fails to capture the richness and subjectivity of what we become directly aware of through reading Faulkner's words. Even the omniscient narrator does not escape subjectivity. We see this in the narrator's word choice and selection of vocabulary, what is described and what is omitted. It is only another point of view from the perspective of the reader. None of these is translatable into the others. We become aware of them, their distinctness, and separation from each other. We acknowledge them and in doing so bring them into our moral world, into our moral consideration. This is something that they, the people depicted, cannot do. Faulkner's novel *shows* us this through its use of form. It is exhibited, pictured for us. We recognize this failure. *That* is the tragedy. Haven't I just said precisely what the novel shows, described the tragedy in words? Well, *not* in so many *words*. The indexical *"that"* is essential. The words can only point like a finger at what we become aware of, what we are acquainted with as exhibited through complex details of the whole work together. *That* cannot be put in fewer, literal terms than the work itself. The words point beyond words to something we cannot articulate, only experience.

How is literature that does this contributing to philosophy or doing philosophy? When we encounter these works, we become aware of complex states of reality that we either were previously unaware of or only vaguely so. We become directly acquainted with them as exhibited to us by the work. Fully conscious or aware of them, we are able to recognize and acknowledge them in others, others separate from us to whom we can extend our moral sensibilities. This knowledge by acquaintance, the acknowledgment it affords, along with the sympathies it allows, are all crucial to our moral understanding of ourselves and others. They are presupposed in our moral motivations and justifications. If philosophy's task includes among its goals the search for knowledge of ourselves and the world necessary to live a good life, then literature that brings us this kind of understanding beyond words plays an essential part in the philosophical project. It does philosophy.

NOTES

1. T. S. Eliot, *The Waste Land*, ed. Michael North, Norton Critical Editions (New York: W. W. Norton & Company, 2001).

2. T. S. Eliot, "Knowledge and Experience in the Philosophy of F.H. Bradley," PhD diss. (Harvard University, completed 1916). Eliot never defended his dissertation.

3. What Hegel actually says is: "Was vernünftig ist, das ist wirklich; und was is wirklich ist, das ist vernünftig" (G. W. F. Hegel, *Grundlinien der Philosophie des Rechts*, [Frankfurt am Main: Suhrkamp, 1970], 24). The German "wirklich" is ambiguous between "real" and "actual." Scholars have good reasons for translating "wirklich" as "actual" in this passage. That is why I refer the one I use as *impressionistic*. For reasons to favor "actual" over "real," see T. M. Knox's notes on his

translation in *Hegel's Philosophy of Right* (Oxford: Oxford University Press, 1952), 302.

4. F. H. Bradley, *Appearance and Reality* (Oxford: Oxford University Press, 1893), 120.

5. J. N. Findlay, *Hegel: A Re-Examination* (New York: Oxford University Press, 1958). Though Findlay's book is on Hegel, this passage is specifically referring to Bradley's view and distinguishing it from Hegel's. Note that defenders of paraconsistent logic will be unimpressed with this reasoning as a defense of the principle of non-contradiction applied to reality. They will simply claim that it begs the question. How do you defend the claim that a contradictory utterance describes nothing without appealing to the principle of non-contradiction?

6. Ludwig Wittgenstein, *Tractatus Logico-Philosophicus*, 2nd edition, trans. D. F. Pears and B. F. McGuiness (London: Routledge & Kegan Paul, 1972), 4.461.

7. Ibid., 4.463.

8. This premise, one antithetical to the *Tractatus*, is reminder enough of how radically Bradley's and Wittgenstein's views diverge. So Wittgenstein: "Thought can never be of anything illogical, since, if it were, we should have to think illogically" (3.03).

9. F. H. Bradley, *Essays on Truth and Reality* (Oxford University Press, 1930), 160–1.

10. Ibid, 173.

11. Ibid.

12. Bradley, *Appearance and Reality*, 21.

13. Ibid., 29.

14. T. S. Eliot, "Dante," in *The Sacred Wood* (London: Methuen & Co., Ltd, 1920), 163. Eliot does not mention Plato, but he does refer to his French contemporary, the poet, Paul Valéry of the same error of exorcising poetry from philosophy, 160.

15. Ibid., 170–71.

16. T. S. Eliot, "Letter to J. H. Woods (28 Jan. 1915)," in *Inventions of the March Hare: Poems 1909–1917*, ed. Christopher Ricks (New York: Harcourt Brace & Co., 1996), 412.

17. T. S. Eliot, "A Prediction with Regard to Three English Authors," in *Inventions of the March Hare*, 412. Originally published in *Vanity Fair*, February 1924.

18. Ibid., 413.

19. Eliot, *The Waste Land*, ll, 433–34. Note that the poem ends without punctuation. It is also worth pointing out that the Sanskrit word, repeated three times at the end, "shantith" connotes an inner peace *beyond understanding* or comprehension.

20. Peter Ackroyd, *T.S. Eliot: A Life* (New York: Simon and Schuster, 1984), 112.

21. Ibid.

22. T. S. Eliot, "Philip Massinger," in *The Sacred Wood*, 125. Eliot completes the sentence with "bad poets deface what they take, and good poets make it into something better, or at least something different."

23. I realize that this is an overstatement. Ezra Pound also pioneered and perfected this technique in his *Cantos* and was a great influence on Eliot. And there may well be poets in other languages and traditions that did much the same thing earlier. More

on the importance of Pound on *The Waste Land* below. See *The Cantos of Ezra Pound,* (New York: New Directions Books, 1981). Pound began publishing the cantos in 1930 and continued adding to them until the end of his life. The first complete volume was published in 1969.

24. Eliot, *The Waste Land*, ll, 203–4, 277–78, 290–91.

25. T. S. Eliot, "The Love Song of J. Alfred Prufrock," in *The Complete Poems and Plays of T.S. Eliot* (Harcourt & Brace, 1980), ll, 103, 109–10.

26. For this fragmentary dialogue see *The Waste Land*, ll, 113–15, 120–24.

27. T. S. Eliot, "Tradition and the Individual Talent," in *The Sacred Wood*, 56.

28. Ackroyd, *T.S. Eliot: A Life*, 120.

29. T. S. Eliot, "Hamlet and His Problems," in *The Sacred Wood*, 100–101.

30. Clive Bell, *Art* (Capricorn Books: New York, 1958), 17–18.

31. Eliot, "Dante," 165.

32. Nelson Goodman coined the technical term *exemplify*. See his *Languages of Art* (Indianapolis: Hackett Publishing Co., 1976), 52–57.

33. Nelson Goodman, *The Ways of Worldmaking* (Indianapolis: Hackett Press, 1978), 102.

34. Ackroyd, *T.S. Eliot, A Life*, 119.

35. There are many readings of it available on the Internet, including Eliot's own. The one I recommend is a reading by Jeremy Irons and Eileen Atkins available on YouTube at https://www.youtube.com/watch?v=sYROFY_Kh8M. The reading by Irons and Atkins first aired on March 30, 2012, on BBC Radio 4.

36. This opens up all kinds of epistemological difficulties that I have not addressed here, such as whether evidence or reasons can ever be non-propositional. I will not take a stand on that here, but simply find it interesting that such examples do indicate a positive answer to that question.

37. Robert Owen Butler, *From Where You Dream*, ed. with an introduction by Janet Burroway (New York: Grove Press, 2005), 108. Walker Percy was not only an important writer in the canon of American Southern literature, he also made original contributions to professional academic philosophy and was an impressive philosopher in his own right. For an interesting example, see his article "Symbol, Consciousness, and Intersubjectivity," *The Journal of Philosophy* 55, no. 15 (July 17, 1958): 631–41.

38. For example, I believe that William Faulkner's *The Sound and the Fury* (New York: Random House, 1984, orig. 1929) and Virginia Woolf's *To the Lighthouse*, forward by Eudora Welty (New York: Harcourt, Brace & Co., 1981, orig. 1927) can, in a way similar to what I provided for *The Waste Land*, be understood as exemplifying or showing something unsayable. Both represent interesting cases of literature as philosophy. More on Faulkner's novel to come.

39. Charles Baxter, "Snow," *New Yorker*, December 19, 1988, 34–39. Reprinted in his collections, *Reflections of a Stranger* and *Gryphon*.

40. Ibid., 34.

41. Ibid., 35.

42. Ibid.

43. Ibid., 36.

44. Ibid.

45. Ibid.
46. Ibid.
47. Ibid., 37.
48. Ibid., 38.
49. Ibid., 39.
50. Ibid.
51. Ibid.

52. Using technical terminology, we might say the middle-age-Russell *stage* is not identical to the twelve-year-old-Russell *stage*. The two Russells are not identical.

53. Goodman, *Ways of Worldmaking*, 104–5.

54. Ibid., 102.

55. T. S. Eliot, "What Dante Means to Me," in *To Criticize the Critic* (Faber and Faber: London, 1965), 125–35.

56. Eliot uses the words "comprehend" and "incomprehensible" (134).

57. Dante Alighieri, *The Divine Comedy*, Book III, *Paradiso*, Canto I, ll, 70–72.

58. Stanley Cavell, "Knowing and Acknowledging," in *Must We Mean What We Say*, updated edition (Cambridge: Cambridge University Press, 2002), 242–43.

59. Ibid., 239.

60. Ibid., 243.

61. Kant analogously talked of the preconditions of our knowledge and moral judgment, certain conditions we had to presuppose to get knowledge or morality off the ground. Our knowledge of the world and other minds presupposed certain transcendental grounds, morality depended on particular practical grounds. We might think of Cavell as suggesting, in a Kantian vein, acknowledgment as an existential ground of knowledge of others and morality.

62. Cavell, "Knowing and Acknowledging," xxiii–xxiv.

63. Jay Parini, *One Matchless Time: A Life of William Faulkner* (New York: HarperCollins Publishers, 2004), 287.

64. Ibid.

65. William Shakespeare, *Macbeth*, Act V, Scene V, ll, 27–28.

66. Donald M. Kartiganer, "*The Sound and the Fury* and the Dislocation of Form," in *William Faulkner's The Sound and the Fury*, ed. Harold Bloom (New York: Chelsea House Publishers, 1988), 23.

67. Ibid., 28.

68. Ibid., 33.

69. Ibid., 35.

Conclusion

HOW PLATO COULD HAVE SETTLED THE ANCIENT QUARREL

Read as a question, the answer is, he couldn't have—not differently from the way he, in fact, did. He feared the threat of the poets' corrupting and degenerating effect on us too much to have done otherwise. Add to that the irrational social and political influence of their popular appeal—that Plato could not allow. Any compromise would have left the poets free to flourish. Poetry would undermine the ascendancy of philosophy and its dialectic method necessary to the creation and preservation of a just state. The poets had to go; he had to forbid their free expression. This much was part of his makeup, an inevitable piece of his puritan personality as well as his philosophy.[1] Yet Plato was himself a great literary writer who bequeathed us some of the finest masterpieces in literary history. He conceived of and rendered his philosophy as drama. His dialogues are all fabrications, with the possible exception of his *Apology*. Though the players were real people, the events almost certainly were fictional. He could write fine poetry when he wanted, and his plays contain some fantastic myths—fantastic in the sense of wonderfully written as well as unbelievable fantasy. There is a simple explanation for why Plato chose to render in words his philosophy as plays. Drama displays the method at work. But his use of myth is harder to explain. Why was he willing to embrace such fictions? I think he could find no other way of *trying* to say what he wanted to say. If he could have said literally what he wanted to say, he would have abandoned these myths for what they were—fictions. Iris Murdoch's diagnosis is insightful: "Plato *wrote* with misgivings, because he knew that truth must live in present consciousness, and cannot live anywhere else."[2] Myth was the best available means for him to reach the consciousness of his audience. But Plato himself was constrained, as we all are, to the consciousness of his time—constrained by the conceptual, semantic, and syntactic limitations of the language of his day. He could not say what he was trying to say in literal terms, so he turned to myth to express it. So, Plato sometimes succumbed to fiction.

Plato himself was only able to conceive of and articulate his great metaphysical and epistemological theories because of fairly recent developments in the syntax and semantics of the Greek of his time. His Greek predecessors could never have thought of it or put it into words. It was inexpressible in their language. As Eric Havelock explained in his classic, *Preface to Plato*: ". . . the terminology which in Plato and Aristotle seeks to define with precision the various operations of the consciousness, in categories which we usually take for granted, had in fact to pass through a considerable period of development before reaching such precision."[3] The developments of the Greek language afforded Plato the language to say much of what he wanted to say. However, rich though it was, this new Greek also limited what he could say and think. Perhaps he was conscious of how much the development and articulation of his philosophy depended on the evolution of the Greek language. Perhaps Plato was not so aware and only had a hint of it when he pushed against the limits of what he could say and turned to myth to show what he could not literally articulate. He might have. If he did, he would have realized that language is evolving in ways we cannot anticipate or expect. The value of poetry and fiction, like myth, would be to push the evolving language into new inexpressible territory. Poetry and fiction, non-literal forms of expression, help drive discovery forward, sometimes showing what cannot literally be said, acquainting us with aspects of reality that we cannot articulate. Had Plato realized this, he could have welcomed in the poets as important, even indispensable, contributors to philosophy.

I am unsure, even doubtful, that Plato could have realized this. But we should. Language is ever evolving. Either it can expand infinitely or it cannot. We may never know which is true. In either case, there are still things unsayable now, and for all we know forever. And in either case, this realm of the unsayable, which we cannot put into literal terms, is as philosophically interesting as it is significant. Great works of poetry and fiction sometimes can lead us, as Beatrice did Dante, into the realm of the unsayable. At the end of his attempt to articulate the nature of reality, Bradley concludes, "It costs little to find that in the end Reality is inscrutable."[4] What is gained is much greater—a philosophy uniquely enriched by fiction. It costs philosophy dearly to deny this contribution and exile poetry and fiction as Plato did. We are left with a philosophy alienated from itself. Its goals and its methods forever at odds. The search for self-knowledge and knowledge of the world around us is constrained to meager methods not fully adequate to the task. Endowed with only the dialectical method of argument and reason, we fail to know who we are and cannot fully acknowledge others. The philosophical goals of the good life and a just society likewise remain out of reach, the ends never entirely understood. Philosophy becomes a tragedy. The exile of poetry and fiction its tragic flaw. Can this be avoided? Yes, perhaps, but this raises another question. As Cavell puts it: "Certainly not so long as philosophy continues, as it has from the first, to demand the banishment of poetry from its republic. Perhaps it could itself become literature. But can it become literature and still know itself?"[5] Plato thought not. I believe otherwise. Only if it recognizes literature's ability to make philosophical contributions can philosophy fully recognize and realize its own ends. It must acknowledge that these philosophical contributions are unique. Works of poetry and fiction can show us subjective aspects of reality only dimly known to us that cannot be put into words. The literary works exhibit them to us and we become aware of them in ourselves and others. We acknowledge them and so expand the moral dimensions of our world and refine our sensibilities. The unsayable insight and awareness the literary arts can lend are necessary to living a good life in a just society. Beatrice guided Dante into paradise to his revelation of the divine. How could Plato have settled the ancient dispute? He could have opened the gates and allowed the poets to lead him through their words to his experience of the unsayable and "let the example suffice any for whom grace reserves that experience." What Plato could have done we should do. Only then will philosophy fully know itself.

NOTES

1. The term 'puritan' for Plato I take from Iris Murdoch, who said: "Plato is of course a puritan. Like all Puritans he hates the theatre . . . the great home of vulgarity" (*The Fire and the Sun* [Oxford: Clarendon Press, 1974], 12–13).

2. Murdoch, *The Fire and the Sun*, 21.

3. Eric C. Havelock, *Preface to Plato* (New York: Grosset & Dunlap, 1963), xi. Havelock credits Snell and von Fritz for first realizing and establishing this conclusion.

4. Bradley, *Appearance and Reality* (Oxford: Oxford University Press, 1893), 488. Of course, I do not endorse Bradley's metaphysics and am only using his words in my own sense.

5. Stanley Cavell, *The Claim of Reason* (Oxford: Oxford University Press, 1979), 496. Cavell's statement is made in the context of discussing Shakespeare's *Othello*, but the point is clearly about the relationship between the literary arts and philosophy in general.

Bibliography

Ackroyd, Peter. *T.S. Eliot: A Life*. New York: Simon and Schuster, 1984.
Alighieri, Dante. *The Divine Comedy, Paradiso*. Translated by Charles S. Singleton. Princeton University Press, 1991.
Anselm. *Proslogion*. In *The Existence of God*, edited by John Hick. New York: MacMillan Publishing, Co., 1964.
Atwood, Margaret. *Negotiating the Dead: A Writer on Writing*. New York: Anchor Books, 2002.
Baxter, Charles. "Snow." *New Yorker*, December 19, 1988.
Bell, Clive. *Art*. New York: Capricorn Books, 1958, orig. 1914.
Bersani, Leo, and Ulysee Dutoit. "'One Big Soul' (*The Thin Red Line*)." In *Forms of Being: Cinema, Aesthetics, and Subjectivity*, 124–78. London: British Film Institute, 2004.
Bradley, F. H. *Appearance and Reality*. Oxford: Oxford University Press, 1893.
———. *Ethical Studies*. 2nd edition. Oxford: Oxford University Press, 1927.
———. *Essays on Truth and Reality*. Oxford: Oxford University Press, 1930.
Butler, Robert Owen. *From Where You Dream: The Process of Writing Fiction*, edited with an introduction by Janet Burroway. New York: Grove Press, 2005.
Cartwright, Nancy. *How the Laws of Physics Lie*. Oxford: Oxford University Press, 1983.
Cavell, Stanley. *The Claim of Reason*. Oxford University Press, 1979.
———. "Knowing and Acknowledging." In *Must We Mean What We Say*, updated edition, 220–45. Cambridge: Cambridge University Press, 2002.
Chomsky, Noam. *Syntactic Structures*. The Hague: Moulton Publishers, 1957.
———. *Aspects of a Theory of Syntax*. Cambridge, MA: M.I.T. Press, 1965.
Cleveland, Timothy. "The Irony of Contingency and Solidarity." *Philosophy* 70, no. 262 (1995): 217–41.
Conee, Earl. "Phenomenal Knowledge." *Australian Journal of Philosophy* 72, no. 2 (1994): 136–50.
Currie, Gregory. *Imagining and Knowing: The Shape of Fiction*. Oxford: Oxford University Press, 2020.
Davidson, Donald. "In Defense of Convention T." In *Inquiries into Truth and Interpretation*, 65–75. Oxford University Press, 1984.

_____. "A Nice Derangement of Epitaphs." In *Truth, Language, and History*, 89–107. New York: Oxford University Press, 2005.

_____. "The Social Aspect of Language." In *Truth, Language, and History*, 109–25. New York: Oxford University Press, 2005.

Dennett, Daniel. "The Milk of Human Intentionality." *Behavioral and Brain Sciences* 3, no. 3 (1980): 428–30.

_____. *Elbow Room*. Cambridge, MA: M.I.T., Press, 1984.

Descartes, Rene. "Letter to Mesland 2 May 1644." In *The Philosophical Writings of Descartes*, 3, translated by John Cottingham et al., 231–36. Cambridge: Cambridge University Press, 1991.

Dummett, Michael. "A Nice Derangement of Epitaphs: Some Comments on Davidson and Hacking." In *Truth and Interpretation*, edited by E. Lepore, 459–76. Oxford University Press, 1986.

Eliot, T. S. "Knowledge and Experience in the Philosophy of F.H. Bradley." PhD diss., Harvard University, 1916.

_____. "Dante." In *The Sacred Wood*, 159–71. London: Methuen & Co., Ltd, 1920.

_____. "Hamlet and His Problems." In *The Sacred Wood*, 95–103. London: Methuen & Co., Ltd, 1920.

_____. "Philip Massinger". In *The Sacred Wood*, 123–43. London: Methuen & Co., Ltd, 1920.

_____. "Tradition and the Individual Talent." In *The Sacred Wood*, 47–59. London: Methuen & Co., Ltd, 1920.

_____. "What Dante Means to Me." In *To Criticize the Critic,* 125–35. London: Faber & Faber, 1965.

_____. "The Love Song of J. Alfred Prufrock." In *The Complete Poems and Plays of T.S. Eliot*, 3–7. New York: Harcourt & Brace, 1980.

_____. "Letter to J.H. Woods (28 Jan. 1915)." In *Inventions of the March Hare: Poems 1909–1917*, edited by Christopher Ricks, 412. New York: Harcourt Brace & Co., 1996.

_____. "A Prediction with Regard to Three English Authors." In *Inventions of the March Hare*, 412.

_____. *The Waste Land*, edited by Michael North. Norton Critical Editions. New York: W. W. Norton & Company, 2001.

Faulkner, William. *The Sound and the Fury*. New, Corrected Edition. New York: Random House, 1984, orig. 1929.

Findlay, J. N. *Hegel: A Re-Examination*. New York: Oxford University Press, 1958.

Fitzgerald, F. Scott. *The Great Gatsby*. New York: MacMillan, 1925.

Frege, Gottlob. *The Foundations of Arithmetic*. Translated by J. L. Austin. Evanston, IL: Northwestern University Press, 1968.

_____. "On Concept and Object." In *Collected Papers on Mathematics, Logic, and Philosophy*, edited by Brian McGuinness, translated by Max Black et al., 182–94. New York: Basil Blackwell, 1984.

Goodman, Nelson. *Languages of Art*. Indianapolis: Hackett Publishing Co., 1976.

_____. *The Ways of Worldmaking*. Indianapolis: Hackett Press, 1978.

Gödel, Kurt. "Ontological Proof." In *Kurt Gödel: Collected Works*, Vol. III, edited by Solomon Feferman et al., 403–4. Oxford: Oxford University Press, 1995.

Hartshorne, Charles. *The Nature of Perfection*. La Salle: Open Court, Press, 1962.

Havelock, Eric C. *Preface to Plato*. New York: Grosset & Dunlap, 1963.

Hegel, G. W. F. *Hegel's Philosophy of Right*. Translated by T. M. Knox. Oxford: Oxford University Press, 1952.

Hempel, Carl. "Studies in the Logic of Explanation." In *Introductory Readings in the Philosophy of Science*, 3rd edition, edited by E. D. Klemke et al., 206–24. New York: Prometheus Books, 1998.

Irons, Jeremy, and Eileen Atkins. Reading of *The Waste Land*. Viewed June 20, 2021. https://www.youtube.com/watch?v=sYROFY_Kh8M. First aired on March 30, 2012, on BBC Radio 4.

Jackson, Frank. "What Mary Didn't Know." *The Journal of Philosophy* 83, no. 5 (May 1986): 291–95.

James, William. *Varieties of Religious Experience*. London: Longmans, Green, 1905.

Jollimore, Troy. "'In the Voiceless Visagelessness.'" In *Melville Among the Philosophers*, edited by Corey McCall and Tom Nurmi, 3-23. Lanham: Lexington Books, 2017.

Jonas, Silvia. *Ineffability and Its Metaphysics*. Palgrave Macmillan, 2016.

Kant, Immanuel. *Critique of Pure Reason*. Translated and edited by Paul Guyer and Allen W. Wood. Cambridge: Cambridge University Press, 1997.

Kartiganer, Donald M. "*The Sound and the Fury* and the Dislocation of Form." In *William Faulkner's The Sound and the Fury (Bloom's Modern Critical Interpretations)*, edited by Harold Bloom. Chelsea House Publications, 2008.

Kennick, W. E. "The Ineffable." *Encyclopedia of Philosophy* 4, edited by Paul Edwards, 181–83. New York: Macmillan Publishing Co., Inc., 1967.

Kitcher, Philip. *Deaths in Venice*. New York: Columbia University Press, 2013.

Kripke, Saul. "Is There a Problem about Substitutional Quantification?" In *Truth and Meaning*, edited by G. Evans & J. McDowell, 325–419. Oxford University Press, 1976.

⸻. *Wittgenstein on Rules and Private Language*. Cambridge, MA: Harvard University Press, 1982.

Kuhn, Thomas. "A Function for Thought Experiments." In *Scientific Revolutions*, edited by Ian Hacking. Oxford: Oxford University Press, 1981.

Lao Tzu. *Tao Te Ching*. Translated by D. C. Lau. New York: Penguin Books, 1963.

Lee, Don. "About Stuart Dybek." *Ploughshares* 24, no. 1. (Spring 1998): 192–98.

Leibniz, Wilhelm. *New Essays Concerning Human Understanding*. Translated by A. G. Langley. New York: MacMillan and Co., 1896.

Lycan, William. *Consciousness and Experience*. Cambridge, MA: M.I.T. Press, 1996.

Mann, Thomas. *Death in Venice*. Translated by Michael Henry Heim, introduction by Michael Cunningham. New York: HarperCollins, 2005, 80–1.

Melville, Herman. *Billy Budd, Sailor*. In *Herman Melville: Billy Budd, Bartleby, and Other Stories*, 243–328. Introduction by Peter Coviello. New York: Penguin Books, 2016.

Mullen, Harryette. *Sleeping with the Dictionary*. Berkeley: University of California Press, 2002.
Murdoch, Iris. *The Fire and the Sun*. Oxford: Clarendon Press, 1974.
Parini, Jay. *One Matchless Time: A Life of William Faulkner*. New York: HarperCollins Publishers, 2004.
Percy, Walker. "Symbol, Consciousness, and Intersubjectivity." *The Journal of Philosophy* 55, no. 15 (July 17, 1958): 631–41.
Plantinga, Alvin. *The Nature of Necessity*. Oxford: Oxford University Press, 1974.
Plato. *Ion*. In *Plato: Complete Works*. Translated by Paul Woodruff, edited by John M. Cooper, 938–49. Indianapolis: Hackett Publishing Company, Inc., 1997.
_____. *Phaedrus*. In *Plato: Complete Works*. Translated by Alexander Nehemas and Paul Woodruff, edited by John M. Cooper, 507–56.
_____. *Republic*. In *Plato: Complete Works*. Translated by G. M. A. Grube, rev. C. D. C. Reeve, edited by John M. Cooper, 972–1223.
Post, Emil. "Introduction to a General Theory of Elementary Propositions." *American Journal of Mathematics* 43, no. 3 (1921): 163–85.
_____. "Finite Combinatory Processes – Formulation 1." *Journal of Symbolic Logic* 1, no. 3 (1936): 103–5.
Pound, Ezra. *The Cantos of Ezra Pound*. New York: New Directions Books, 1981.
Prichard, H. A. "Does Moral Philosophy Rest on a Mistake?" In *Moral Obligation*. Oxford: Oxford University Press, 1949.
Quine, W. V. "Two Dogmas of Empiricism." In *From a Logical Point of View*, 2nd edition, revised, 20–46. Cambridge, MA: Harvard University Press, 1980.
Rawls, John. "Two Concepts of Rules." *Philosophical Review* 64, no. 1 (1955): 3–32.
Russell, Bertrand. *The Problems of Philosophy*. Oxford University Press, 1912.
Smart, J. J. C. and Bernard Williams. *Utilitarianism For & Against*. Cambridge University Press, 1971.
Syme, Rachel. "On the Nose: How to Make Sense of Smells." *New Yorker*, February 1, 2021.
Tarski, Alfred. "The Semantic Conception of Truth and the Foundations of Semantics." *Philosophy and Phenomenological Research* 4, no. 3 (1944): 341–76.
_____. "The Concept of Truth in Formalized Languages." In *Logic, Semantics, and Metamathematics*. 2nd edition, edited by John Corcoran, translated by J. H. Woodger, 152–278. Indianapolis: Hackett Publishing Co., 1983.
Walker, Mark. "On the Intertranslatability of All Natural Languages." Unpublished manuscript.
Wallace, David Foster. "Good Old Neon." In *Oblivion: Stories*, 141–81. New York: Little Brown and Company, 2004.
_____. "Laughing with Kafka." *Log*, no. 22, The Absurd (Spring/Summer 2011): 47–50.
Wilcox, Leonard. "Don DeLillo's *Underworld* and the Return of the Real." *Contemporary Literature* 43, no. 1 (Spring 2002): 120–37.
Williamson, Timothy. *Modal Logic as Metaphysics*. Oxford University Press, 2013.

Wittgenstein, Ludwig. *Tractatus Logico-Philosophicus.* 2nd edition, translated by D. F. Pears and B. F. McGuiness. London: Routledge & Kegan Paul, 1972, orig. 1922.
_____. *Philosophical Investigations*. 3rd edition, translated by G. E. M. Anscombe. New York: Macmillan Co., Inc., 1958.
Woolf, Virginia. *To the Lighthouse*. Forward by Eudora Welty. New York: Harcourt, Brace & Co., 1981, orig. 1927.

Index

absolute idealism, 83
acknowledge/acknowledging (as opposed to knowing) 6–7, 33–34, 100–101, 105, 110–111
Ackroyd, Peter, 88, 90
Acts, 79n29
Aeschylus, 9
Alighieri, Dante, 7, 32, 33, 86, 88–92, 98–100, 102
Anselm, 42, 56n17
Antony & Cleopatra, 89
appearance, 12, 14–15, 27, 84–85
Appearance and Reality, 37n4, 83, 86, 111n4
Aristophanes, 9
Aristotle, 23n18, 54, 110
Atkins, Eileen, 107n35
Atwood, Margaret, 13, 22n5
Augustine of Hippo, 89

Baudelaire, Charles, 89
Baxter, Charles, 7, 94–98, 100
Beethoven, Ludwig van, 1
Bell, Clive, 91, 107n30
Berra, Yogi, 73–74, 76
Bersani, Leo, 1–2, 7n1
Billy Budd, 6, 63–70, 78n19
Bleak House, 63, 68
Boswell, Robert, 20

Bradley, F.H., 21, 25, 39, 43, 66, 79n39, 83–91, 93, 106n5, 110, 111n4
Bromhall, Kyle, xiii
Buddha, 83, 89–90
Buddhist logicians, 21
Butler, Robert Owen, 19, 93

Cartwright, Nancy, 18
Cavell, Stanley, xii, 6–7, 33–34, 98, 100–101, 108n61, 111
Chappelle, Dave, 3
Chomsky, Noam, 47, 71, 80n64
Cleveland, Timothy, 78n11
coherentism, 61
Colapietro, Vince, xiii
Coltrane, John, 1
complex emotion, 1, 87, 92–94, 96–97, 102
complex states: first-person consciousness, 92; psychological, 87, 93–94, 97, 100, 104; reality, 105
Conee, Earl, 31, 35
The Confessions, 89
consequentialism, 66–67, 68, 79n39
  rule consequentialism, 66
contradiction, 53, 62, 84–85, 106n5
covering-law model, 18
Critique of Pure Reason, 25
Cummings, E.E., xii

119

Currie, Gregory, 17, 34, 68, 69–70, 79n44

Davidson, Donald, 45–46, 71–75, 77, 80n62
Da Vinci, Leonardo 1
Davis, Miles, 1
Death in Venice, 14–15
DeLillo, Don, 3
Dennett, Daniel, 69
deontological intuitions, 68
Descartes, Rene, 57n33
dialectic/dialectical method, 9–10, 13, 61, 63, 66, 84, 109–110
Dickens, Charles, 86
The Divine Comedy, 86, 88, 91–92, 99, 100
Dummett, Michael, 80n62
Dutoit, Ulysse, 1–2
Dybek, Stuart, 21

Earl of Leicester, 89
Ecclesiastes, 89
Einstein, Albert, 53–54, 69, 79n44
Eliot, T.S., xiii, 7, 32–33, 83, 85–87, 88–94, 98, 99, 100, 102–104, 105n2
Elizabeth 1 of England, 89
Euripides, 9
exhibit (in fiction), 6, 32, 34, 86–87, 93–94, 97, 99–102, 104–105, 111
Ezekiel, 89

family resemblance, 69, 80n47
Faulkner, William, xii, 7, 102, 104–105
Findlay, J.N., 84, 106n5
The Fire Sermon, 89
first law of falling bodies, 18–19, 68
first-person knowledge, 5
first-person experience/consciousness, 5–6, 28, 31–32, 34–36, 92, 100
Fitzgerald, F. Scott, 17, 30
formal correlative, 91, 102
foundationalism, 61
Frazer, James, 89
Frege, Gottlob, 16, 22n10, 48

Freud, Sigmund, 20; psychoanalysis, 3, 20
From Ritual to Romance, 89

Galilei, Galileo, 69
General laws of the causal type, 18
genetic fallacy, 15, 60–61, 78n10
God: in Kantian philosophy, 27; knowledge of, 31, 42; experience of, 43; expressibility, 44–45, 51–53
The Golden Bough, 89
Goldsmith, Oliver, 89
good life, the, 11
Goodman, Nelson, 92, 93, 98
Gödel, Kurt, 42
The Great Gatsby, 17
Grob, Kristina, xiii
Gross, Terry, 20

Hartshorne, Charles, 42
Havelock, Eric C., 111n3
Hegel, Georg Wilhelm Friedrich, 61, 83–84, 86, 88, 105n3
Hempel, Carl, 18
Hesse, Hermann, 89
Hodges-Kluck, Jana, xiii
Homer, 9, 11, 13
Hume, David: bundle theory, 90

imagining (vs. believing), 17, 79n44
incommensurability, 54
instrumentalism, 19
intuition (epistemological), 26–27, 31–32, 55n13, 62
intuition pumps, 69, 70
Ion, 11
Irons, Jeremy, 107n35
Isaiah, 89

Jackson, Frank, 29
James, William, 31, 45
Jesus, 13
Jollimore, Troy, 62
Jonas, Silvia, 39–43
Joyce, James, 88

Index

Kafka, Franz, 3
Kant, Immanuel, 25–27, 39, 43, 48, 85, 100, 108n61
Kartiganer, Donald, 103, 104
Kennick, W.E., 39
Kitcher, Philip, 6, 22n9, 59–61, 63, 68, 78n4-5
Knowledge: by acquaintance, 5, 27, 30–32, 34–35, 37, 38n19, 44, 91–92, 100–101, 105; de re, 32; moral/spiritual, 15, 108n61; non-propositional, 5, 32, 34, 41, 44, 92, 101, 107n36; of the world, 10, 16, 26, 110; of self ("self-knowledge"), 10, 16, 101, 105, 110; of the nature of things, 4, 12; propositional, 29–31, 72, 101; religious, 42
Knox, T. M., 105n3
Kripke, Saul, 80n64
Kuhn, Thomas, 69

Leary, Timothy, 43
Lee, Don, 21
Leibniz, Gottfried Wilhelm, 42
limits of language, xi, 6, 48, 50–52, 54–55, 97, 109–110
logic: modal, first-order 47; paraconsistent, 106n5
logical positivism, 18
Lycan, William, 28

Macbeth, 103
malaprop/malapropism, 71, 73–77, 81n69
Malick, Terrence, xii, 1
Mann, Thomas, 14, 15
Melville, Hermann, 6, 20, 23n24, 63–64
Meno, 17
Metamorphoses, 99
Milton, John, 89
modal realism, 23n15
moral reality, 2, 70, 101
moral residue, 63, 68, 87
Mullen, Harryette, 7, 74–77
Murdoch, Iris, 111n1

Mylae, 89
myth, 9, 10, 13–14, 89, 109–110

Nagarjuna, 21
Nagel, Thomas, 17, 31–32, 34–35
Neurath, Otto, 61
Newtonian physics, 53
Newton, Isaac, 54
noumena, 26–27

objective: representation, 2; knowledge, 31, 35–36; reality, 26, 32
objective correlative, 91
omnipotent, 44, 51
omniscient, 44, 45, 103–105
ontological argument, 42, 56n18
Ovid, 89, 99

Parini, Jay, 102
passing theory, 73–74
paradox: regarding the unsayable, 1, 5, 7, 21; Frege on the concept of horse, 48
Percy, Walker, 93
Phaedrus, 13, 14
phenomena (Kantian), 26
phenomenal experience, 28, 35
Philosophical Investigations, 44, 73, 80n47
Picasso, Pablo, 1
picture theory of meaning, 2, 48–50
Plantinga, Alvin, 42
Plato: on beauty, 14; on beliefs vs. causes, 15–16, 60–61, 63; on dialectic method, 13, 61; on myths, 109–110; on poets, 4, 5, 7, 10–17, 19, 21, 59, 86, 98, 101, 109–111
platonic entity (language as), 52
Ploughshares, 21
Pollock, Jackson, 1
Poncé, Michael, xiii
Post, Emil, 71
Pound, Ezra, 90, 92, 106n23
Prichard, H. A., 64

prior theory, 73
problem of other minds, 33
psychologism, 16, 61

qualia, 35–36
quantum mechanics, 53
quasi-beliefs, 17
Quine, W. V., 36, 61, 98

Rawls, John, 66
reasons (justification), xii, 13, 15–19, 59, 60–63, 78n10-11, 92, 107n36
relativity theory, 53, 69
religious experience, 42–43
Republic, 9, 12, 16
revelation: religious, xi, 5, 31–32, 104; of the divine, 7, 31, 111
Rogers, Fred, 77
Roget's Thesaurus, 76
Rothko, Mark, 1
Russell, Bertrand, 30, 32, 38n19

The Sacred Wood, 98–99
Sappho, 9, 89
scientific realism, 19
scientific knowledge, 53–54
Searle, John, 69
semantic expansion, xii, 46–47, 51–52, 54, 74, 83
sense perception, 40
Shakespeare, William, 89, 103
Sheridan, Richard, 74
The Sound and the Fury, xii, 7, 102
skepticism, 33–34
Shostakovich, Dmitri 1
significant form, 91
Sleeping With the Dictionary, 7, 74
Smart, J.J.C., 79n35
Socrates, 13, 14, 17, 66
Sophocles, 9
Spenser, Edmund, 89

states of consciousness, 5–6
stream of consciousness, 103
subjective: aspects of reality, 31, 111; experience, 5, 29, 32, 103; representation, 2, 3
Syme, Rachel, 28–29
Syntactic Structures, 71

Tarski, Alfred, 46–47, 52, 71–72
The Thin Red Line, 1–2, 7
thought experiments, 6, 63, 68–69
Tractatus Logico-Philosophicus, 21, 50
transcendental argument, 43–44, 50, 54–55
transhuman, 100
trasumanar, 100
Tzu, Lao, 38n24

Ulysses, 88
understanding (philosophical), xi, xii, 4, 13, 15, 19
Underworld, 3
universal grammar, 47
The Upanishads, 83, 89

Valéry, Paul, 106n14
Vanity Fair, 87
Verlaine, Paul, 89
Vermeer, Johannes, 1
Vessel, Jean-Paul, xiii
Virgil, 89

Wagner, Richard, 89
Walker, Mark, xii, 45–46
Wallace, David Foster, 2, 25, 27, 56n24
Weston, Jesse, 89
The Waste Land, 7, 83, 86–94, 100, 102, 104, 106n19
Wilcox, Leonard, 7n6
Williams, Bernard, 66
Williamson, Timothy, 47, 48

Wittgenstein, Ludwig, 2, 5, 21, 25–26, 39, 43–45, 48–50, 56n24, 69, 73, 75, 80n47, 80n64, 85, 91, 106n8

Woolf, Virginia, 107n38

Yogism, 73–75

About the Author

Timothy Cleveland is professor and head of the Department of Philosophy at New Mexico State University and the author of *Trying Without Willing: An Essay in the Philosophy of Mind*.

www.ingramcontent.com/pod-product-compliance
Lightning Source LLC
Chambersburg PA
CBHW020127010526
44115CB00008B/1012